# frame>by>frame
# baking

# frame>by>frame
# baking

## a visual step-by-step cookbook

This edition published in 2010
LOVE FOOD is an imprint of Parragon Books Ltd

Parragon
Queen Street House
4 Queen Street
Bath BA1 1HE, UK

ISBN: 978-1-4454-0595-7

Printed in China

Cover and internal design by Talking Design
Photography by Mike Cooper
Home economy by Lincoln Jefferson
Introduction and cover text by Linda Doeser
New recipes by Christine France

**Notes for the Reader**
This book uses both metric and imperial measurements. Follow the same units of measurement throughout; do not mix metric and imperial. All spoon measurements are level: teaspoons are assumed to be 5 ml, and tablespoons are assumed to be 15 ml. Unless otherwise stated, milk is assumed to be full fat, eggs and individual vegetables are medium, and pepper is freshly ground black pepper.

The times given are an approximate guide only. Preparation times differ according to the techniques used by different people and the cooking times may also vary from those given. Optional ingredients, variations or serving suggestions have not been included in the calculations.

Recipes using raw or very lightly cooked eggs should be avoided by infants, the elderly, pregnant women, convalescents and anyone suffering from an illness. Pregnant and breastfeeding women are advised to avoid eating peanuts and peanut products. Sufferers from nut allergies should be aware that some of the ready-made ingredients used in the recipes in this book may contain nuts. Always check the packaging before use.

# contents

introduction                              06
cakes & traybakes                         16
pastries                                  68
small cakes & biscuits 120
breads                                   170
index                                    222

# introduction

**This magnificent cookbook with its profusion of beautiful and immensely useful photographs will prove to be an invaluable addition to any cook's bookshelf. The recipes are clear, easy to follow, beautifully illustrated and simply scrumptious, so whatever your level of expertise in the kitchen you are virtually guaranteed success every time.**

Every recipe starts with a photograph of all the ingredients but this is more than just a pretty picture or – even less helpful – a montage that is not to scale so that a pear appears to be the same size as an egg. Instead, it serves as a handy way of checking that you have everything ready before you start cooking. Just comparing the picture with the ingredients arranged on your own worktop or kitchen table will ensure that you haven't missed anything out and when it's time to add the glacé cherries, for example, you have already quartered them as specified in the ingredients list. If you're uncertain about how thinly to slice fruit or how dark to toast nuts, a glance at the photograph will provide an instant answer.

Each short and straightforward step of the method is clearly explained without any jargon or difficult technical terms. Once again, what you see in the photograph is what you should expect to see in front of you. Not only is this reassuring for the novice cook; those with more experience will find it a helpful reminder of

the little touches that can easily be overlooked. Each recipe ends with a mouth-watering photograph of the finished cake, biscuits, tart or loaf.

## Why you need this book

Even some quite experienced cooks find 'baking' a daunting prospect and think it's sure to be difficult. Yet the word baking encompasses many different kinds of products from biscuits to bread and a variety of different techniques from creamed sponge cakes to choux pastry. They can't all be impossibly difficult and demanding and, in fact, most are astonishingly easy.

In this book there are 60 easy-to-follow recipes for cakes, traybakes, sweet and savoury pastries, biscuits and bread – some traditional family favourites and others with a contemporary twist, some for special occasions and others for everyday treats. All of them are straightforward and, by using the unique frame-by-frame guide, even the novice cook will find they're figuratively and literally a piece of cake.

**>1 >2 >3**

# top tips for easy baking

> Read all the way through the recipe – ingredients list and method – before you start, so that you know exactly what you will need. Scrabbling about at the back of the storecupboard to find a rarely used ingredient or moving half a dozen other utensils to reach the one you need in the middle of preparing a cake batter or bread dough is, at best, exasperating and, at worst, liable to spoil it.

> Except when you are making pastry dough by the rubbing-in method, collect all your ingredients together, including anything that is normally stored in the refrigerator, at least half an hour before you start cooking to bring them to room temperature. Eggs are particularly important because if they are too cold when they are added, they tend to curdle. Remove mixing bowls from the cupboard to bring them to room temperature too.

> When making pastry dough, collect the dry ingredients and any filling ingredients together ready for use and put a jug of water in the refrigerator to chill. (Keeping the dough cold is essential for crisp results.)

> Accurate measurement of the ingredients is more important for baking than for any other kind of cooking. Weigh dry ingredients on reliable kitchen scales and measure liquids in a measuring jug or, for small quantities, standard measuring spoons. Use medium eggs unless another size is specified in the recipe.

> Always preheat the oven to the specified temperature. An oven that is not hot enough will cause baked goods to sink, while one that is too hot can cause them to crack. If you're unsure about the reliability of your thermostat, invest in an oven thermometer and use that to check the temperature.

> The type of flour used for baking is important, and substituting one for another may produce disappointing results. Plain flour is used for pastry dough and anything that does not need a raising

agent. Self-raising flour has added baking powder and is used for many different kinds of cakes. Strong bread flour has a high gluten content that produces an elastic dough when kneaded. Wholemeal flour is made from the whole grain and produces a denser, nuttier, slightly more chewy texture than white flour. If you do want to use it – in pastry dough, for example – substitute it for only half the quantity of white flour in the recipe. Whatever flour you are using, it is always worth sifting it to add air and remove any lumps, even if it is described as ready-sifted on the packet.

> Bread recipes often require yeast and may specify using hand-hot liquid. Yeast works best at a temperature of 21–36°C/70–97°F. Do not use hotter water as this will kill the yeast and prevent it from producing the gases that cause the bread to rise.

> Always use the size and shape of baking tin specified in the recipe. A tin that is too large will result in cracks and airholes and one that is too small is likely to cause the cake or loaf to burn.

> Follow the recipe instructions for cooling. Some cakes and biscuits are fragile and should be left for a short while in the tin to firm up slightly before turning out on to a wire cooling rack. Others should be turned out on to the rack immediately after they have been removed from the oven or the base will become soggy. Heavy cakes are usually allowed to cool completely in the tin.

# time-saving shortcuts

> Melt chocolate in the microwave oven. Break it into pieces and put it into a microwave-proof bowl. Heat on MEDIUM for 10 seconds, then stir. Return to the oven and heat for another 10 seconds before checking and stirring again – even when it's melted it will hold its shape so you cannot tell if it's ready just by looking at it. White chocolate should be heated on LOW.

> Toast nuts in the microwave to avoid burning. Spread out 4 tablespoons nuts on a microwave-proof plate and cook on HIGH for 5 minutes.

> All is not lost if you have forgotten to remove the butter from the refrigerator in advance – just microwave on HIGH for 15–20 seconds.

> The easiest way to peel fruits such as nectarines and peaches, as well as tomatoes, is to slit their skins, put them into a heatproof bowl and pour in boiling water to cover. Leave to stand for 30–60 seconds and drain. The skins will slip off much more easily.

> When measuring small quantities of something sticky such as honey or syrup, stand the spoon in hot water for a minute. It will then drop off the spoon easily.

> If dough is sticky, even after chilling in the refrigerator, roll it out between sheets of baking parchment or clingfilm. You can use the bottom sheet to help you transfer it to the baking sheet.

# useful equipment

> **Kitchen scales:** It is important to be precise when weighing ingredients for baking. Electronic scales are the most accurate but the batteries do need replacing quite frequently. Spring scales are very easy to use, while old-fashioned balance scales are accurate but a little more fiddly.

> **Measuring jugs:** These are available in a variety of shapes and sizes. It is easier to measure liquids accurately using a tall, thin jug than a short fat one and a clear jug is more useful than an opaque one.

> **Measuring spoons:** Ordinary spoons vary in size so you will need at least one set of standard measuring spoons. As they are inexpensive, it's worth buying several sets so that you don't have to keep washing them.

> **Mixing bowls:** You will need a selection of different sizes – large for mixing dough and cake batters, medium for measuring out ingredients and small for melting chocolate, mixing icing, etc. Both heatproof glass and ceramic bowls are useful; remember that metal bowls cannot be used in the microwave.

> **Sieves:** A strong fine wire sieve is essential for sifting dry ingredients to aerate them. A small sieve is useful for dusting cakes and biscuits with icing sugar.

> **Spoons and spatulas:** A set of wooden spoons in different sizes is invaluable for all kinds of tasks from stirring a melted chocolate mixture in a hot pan to pressing fruit through a sieve. A long-handled metal spoon is perfect for folding dry ingredients into a whisked mixture. Flexible rubber or plastic spatulas, available in a variety of sizes, are useful for stirring, mixing, folding and scraping all the cake batter out of the bowl.

> **Pastry blender:** This tool is used for working fat into flour rather than using your fingertips. It helps to keep the mixture cool but is not essential.

> **Whisks:** A hand-held balloon whisk is useful for many tasks from aerating egg whites to whisking cream. A hand-held electric whisk takes the hard work out of these processes, is strong enough to cream butter and sugar mixtures and can be used in a hot pan.

> **Rolling pin:** These can be made of wood, glass, marble or plastic and some can be filled with cold water to keep dough cool. Choose a heavy rolling pin that will do the job without your having to press down and so distort the dough.

> **Pastry board:** Marble is the best surface because it keeps the dough cool and requires only a very light dusting of flour. Wood is popular and, as it's a poor conductor of heat, it's also good for rolling out biscuit doughs.

13

> **Biscuit and pastry cutters:** These are available in a wide range of sizes and shapes with plain or fluted edges. Metal cutters produce a cleaner edge than plastic ones.

> **Cake tins:** Heavy gauge cake tins distribute the heat evenly and prevent scorching. It is a matter of personal choice whether you prefer them with a non-stick lining. Round tins are used more often than other shapes, but always check the recipe. The most useful sizes are shallow 20-cm/8-inch sandwich tins for sponge cakes and deep 23–25-cm/9–10-inch tins for larger cakes. A Swiss roll tin is rectangular and very shallow, while a slightly deeper rectangular tin may be used for traybakes. Other specialist tins include springform tins, which have a clip on the side, making it easy to remove the tin from very fragile cakes, and angel cake tins with a central tube projecting above the rim.

> **Loaf tins:** Bread is quite often baked on a flat baking sheet as the dough is dense enough to retain its shape. When a tin is used, the base and sides of the loaf are contained, so the dough expands upwards, creating a denser crumb and crisp crust. Loaf tins are usually rectangular and popular sizes are 17 x 11 x 8 cm/6½ x 4¼ x 3¼ inches and 19 x 12 x 9 cm/7½ x 4½ x 3½ inches. They are available with non-stick linings.

> **Bun, muffin and tart tins:** Available with a non-stick coating if you prefer, bun tins are perfect for small cakes and individual sweet or savoury tarts. A 12-cup tray is a useful size. Muffin trays have deep cups with flared sides that encourage the dough to rise. Large tarts can be made in ovenproof glass or ceramic dishes, but metal ones distribute the heat more quickly and evenly. They are usually round and may be plain or fluted and with or without a removable base. They are available in a range of sizes; deeper tins are best for tarts that require a firm crust to support a cream- or egg-based filling, while shallower tins are ideal for glazed fruit tarts.

> **Baking sheets and trays:** It is best to buy heavy sheets and trays as they do not buckle or wobble, and distribute the heat evenly. Baking sheets usually have a slightly sloping edge to make it easier to lift them and are used for many kinds of loaves, pastries and some types of biscuits. Baking trays have a rim around the entire edge to prevent runny mixtures from falling off.

> **Cooling rack:** Wire racks are made in a wide variety of shapes and sizes. They let air circulate around a cake or biscuits, preventing trapped moisture from making them soggy while they cool.

>1

>2

>3

# cakes & traybakes

>4

>5

>6

# classic cherry cake

serves 8

**ingredients**

200 g/7 oz unsalted butter,
  plus extra for greasing
250 g/9 oz glacé cherries,
  quartered

85 g/3 oz ground almonds
200 g/7 oz plain flour
1 tsp baking powder
200 g/7 oz caster sugar
3 large eggs

finely grated rind and juice
  of 1 lemon
6 sugar cubes, crushed

> **1** Preheat the oven to 180°C/350°F/ Gas Mark 4. Grease and line a 20-cm/8-inch round cake tin.

> **2** Stir together the cherries, almonds and 1 tablespoon of the flour. Sift the remaining flour into a separate bowl with the baking powder.

> **3** Cream together the butter and sugar until light and fluffy. Gradually add the eggs, beating hard, until evenly mixed.

> **4** Add the flour mixture and fold lightly and evenly into the creamed mixture with a metal spoon. Add the cherry mixture, fold in evenly, then fold in the lemon rind and juice.

19

> **5** Spoon the mixture into the prepared tin and sprinkle with the crushed sugar cubes. Bake in the preheated oven for 1–1¼ hours, or until risen and golden brown and shrinking from the sides of the tin.

> **6** Leave to cool in the tin for about 15 minutes, then turn out onto a wire rack to cool completely.

Cut into slices and serve as
a mid-morning treat.

# chocolate fudge cake

**serves 8**

**ingredients**

175 g/6 oz unsalted butter,
  softened, plus extra for
  greasing
175 g/6 oz golden caster sugar
3 eggs, beaten

3 tbsp golden syrup
40 g/1½ oz ground almonds
175 g/6 oz self-raising flour
pinch of salt
40 g/1½ oz cocoa powder

**icing**

225 g/8 oz plain chocolate,
  broken into pieces
55 g/2 oz dark muscovado
  sugar

225 g/8 oz unsalted butter,
  diced
5 tbsp evaporated milk
½ tsp vanilla extract

>1 Preheat the oven to 180°C/350°F/Gas Mark 4. Grease and line two 20-cm/8-inch sandwich tins.

>2 For the icing, place the ingredients in a heavy-based saucepan. Heat gently, stirring constantly, until melted.

>3 Pour into a bowl and leave to cool. Cover and chill for 1 hour, or until spreadable.

>4 For the cake, place the butter and sugar in a bowl and beat together until light and fluffy. Gradually beat in the eggs. Stir in the golden syrup and almonds.

**>5** Sift the flour, salt and cocoa powder into a separate bowl, then fold into the mixture. Add a little water, if necessary, to make a dropping consistency.

**>6** Spoon the mixture into the prepared tins and bake in the preheated oven for 30–35 minutes, or until springy to the touch and a skewer inserted in the centre comes out clean.

**>7** Cool in the tins for 5 minutes, then turn out onto a wire rack to cool completely.

**>8** When the cakes are cold, sandwich them together with half the icing. Spread the remaining icing over the top and sides of the cake, swirling it to give a frosted appearance.

Cut into slices and serve.

# victoria sponge cake

**serves 8**

### ingredients

175 g/6 oz butter, softened,
   plus extra for greasing
175 g/6 oz self-raising flour
1 tsp baking powder
175 g/6 oz golden caster sugar
3 eggs
icing sugar, sifted, for dusting

### filling

3 tbsp raspberry jam
300 ml/10 fl oz double cream,
   whipped
16 fresh strawberries, halved

**>1** Preheat the oven to 180°C/350°F/
Gas Mark 4. Grease and base-line two
20-cm/8-inch sandwich tins.

**>2** Sift the flour and baking powder into a
bowl and add the butter, sugar and eggs.
Mix together, then beat well until smooth.
Divide the mixture evenly between the
prepared tins and smooth the surfaces.

Dust with icing sugar and serve.

**>3** Bake in the preheated oven for 25–30 minutes, or until well risen and golden brown. Cool in the tins for 5 minutes, then turn out onto a wire rack to cool completely.

**>4** Sandwich together with jam, cream and strawberry halves.

# banana coconut loaf cake

**makes 1 loaf**

**ingredients**

90 ml/3 fl oz sunflower oil, plus
  extra for greasing
250 g/9 oz plain flour
1½ tsp baking powder

200 g/7 oz caster sugar
55 g/2 oz desiccated coconut
2 eggs
2 ripe bananas, mashed
125 ml/4 fl oz soured cream

1 tsp vanilla extract
long shred coconut, toasted,
  to decorate

> **1** Preheat the oven to 180°C/350°F/Gas Mark 4. Grease and line a 1-litre/1¾ pint loaf tin.

> **2** Sift together the flour and baking powder in a large bowl.

> **3** Stir in the sugar and coconut.

> **4** Beat together the eggs, oil, bananas, cream and vanilla extract in a large bowl.

29

**>5** Stir into the dry ingredients, mixing until evenly combined.

**>6** Spoon into the prepared tin, levelling with a palette knife.

**>7** Bake in the preheated oven for about 1 hour or until risen, firm and golden brown.

**>8** Cool in the tin for 15 minutes, then turn out onto a wire rack to cool completely.

Decorate with shreds of coconut and serve.

# rich almond cake

**serves 8**

**ingredients**

butter, for greasing
250 g/9 oz ricotta cheese
4 eggs, separated

1 tsp almond essence
175 g/6 oz golden caster sugar
250 g/9 oz ground almonds
finely grated rind of 1 lime

toasted flaked almonds,
 to decorate
icing sugar, sifted, for dusting

>1 Preheat the oven to 150°C/300°F/ Gas Mark 2. Grease and line a 23-cm/9-inch round cake tin.

>2 Beat together the ricotta, egg yolks, almond essence and sugar. Stir in the almonds and lime rind.

>3 Whisk the egg whites in a clean bowl until they form soft peaks.

>4 Fold the whites lightly into the ricotta mixture, using a large metal spoon.

>5 Spread the mixture in the tin and bake in the preheated oven for 50–60 minutes, until firm and lightly browned.

>6 Cool the cake in the tin for 10 minutes, then turn out onto a wire rack and sprinkle with flaked almonds.

Dust with icing sugar and serve.

# double chocolate mint sponge

**serves 8**

## ingredients

175 g/6 oz unsalted butter,
  softened, plus extra for
  greasing
150 g/5½ oz plain flour
2 tbsp cocoa powder
1 tbsp baking powder
175 g/6 oz caster sugar
3 eggs, beaten
1 tbsp milk
40 g/1½ oz chocolate mint
  sticks, chopped
140 g/5 oz chocolate spread,
  plus extra to drizzle
chocolate mint sticks
  to decorate

>1  Preheat the oven to 180°C/350°F/
Gas Mark 4. Grease and line two
20-cm/8-inch sandwich tins.

>2  Sift the flour, cocoa and baking
powder into a bowl and beat in the
butter, sugar and eggs, mixing until
smooth. Stir in the milk and chocolate
mint pieces.

Decorate the cake with chocolate mint sticks.

> **3** Spread the mixture into the tins. Bake in the preheated oven for 25–30 minutes, until risen and firm. Cool in the tins for 2 minutes, then turn out onto a wire rack to cool completely.

> **4** Sandwich the cakes together with chocolate spread. Gently warm a little of the spread and drizzle it over the top.

# orange madeira ring

**serves 8**

## ingredients

175 g/6 oz unsalted butter, plus extra for greasing

1 tbsp golden syrup (plus extra for drizzling, if liked)

2 medium oranges

175 g/6 oz caster sugar

3 eggs, beaten

115 g/4 oz plain flour

115 g/4 oz self-raising flour

finely grated rind of 1 orange

2–3 tbsp orange juice

> **1** Preheat the oven to 160°C/325°F/Gas Mark 3. Grease a 1.5-litre/2¾-pint ring cake tin and spoon the syrup into the base.

> **2** Cut all the white peel and pith from the oranges and slice.

> **3** Arrange the orange slices over the syrup in the tin.

> **4** Cream together the butter and sugar until pale and fluffy.

**>5** Gradually beat in the eggs, beating well after each addition.

**>6** Sift the flours into the mixture and fold in, adding the orange rind and enough juice to make a soft consistency.

**>7** Spoon the mixture into the tin and smooth the surface.

**>8** Bake in the preheated oven for 45–55 minutes or until risen, golden and firm. Cool in the tin for 10 minutes, then turn out onto a wire rack to cool completely.

The cake can be served cold,
or warm with extra golden
syrup drizzled over.

# caramel peach gâteau

**serves 6–8**

### ingredients

175 g/6 oz unsalted butter,
  softened, plus extra for
  greasing
175 g/6 oz light muscovado
  sugar

3 eggs, beaten
1 tsp vanilla extract
175 g/6 oz self-raising flour
½ tsp baking powder
2 tbsp milk

### filling

2 tbsp maple syrup
200 ml/7 fl oz thick crème
  fraîche (40% fat)
3 ripe peaches, thinly sliced

>1 Preheat the oven to 180°C/350°F/Gas Mark 4. Grease and base-line two 23-cm/9-inch round sandwich tins.

>2 Place the butter, sugar, eggs and vanilla extract in a bowl and sift over the flour and baking powder.

>3 Beat with an electric mixer until smooth, then add milk to make a soft consistency.

>4 Divide the mixture between the tins and spread evenly.

**>5** Bake in the preheated oven for 25–30 minutes, until firm and golden. Cool in the tins for 2 minutes, then turn out onto a wire rack to cool completely.

**>6** Swirl 1 tbsp maple syrup into the crème fraîche and spread half over each cake.

**>7** Arrange half the peach slices over one cake and top with the remaining cake, crème fraîche side down.

**>8** Arrange the remaining peach slices over the top of the cake.

Brush the peach slices with maple syrup just before serving. Serve the cake on the day of filling.

# honey & almond cake

serves 12–16

## ingredients

150 g/5½ oz unsalted butter,
 plus extra for greasing
115 g/4 oz light muscovado
 sugar
175 g/6 oz clear honey
1 tbsp lemon juice
2 eggs, beaten
200 g/7 oz self-raising flour
15 g/½ oz flaked almonds
warmed honey, to glaze

> **>1** Preheat the oven to 180°C/350°F/Gas Mark 4. Grease and line a 20-cm/8-inch deep cake tin.

> **>2** Place the butter, sugar, honey and lemon juice in a saucepan and stir over a medium heat, without boiling, until melted and smooth.

Brush with the warmed honey and cut into slices to serve.

>3 Remove the pan from the heat and quickly beat in the eggs with a wooden spoon. Sift in the flour and stir lightly with a metal spoon. Pour into the prepared tin and scatter the almonds over the top.

>4 Bake in the preheated oven for 35–40 minutes, until risen, firm and golden brown. Cool in the tin for 15 minutes, then turn out onto a wire rack to cool completely.

# coffee & walnut roulade

**serves 6**

### ingredients
butter or oil, for greasing
3 eggs
1 egg white
115 g/4 oz golden caster sugar,
  plus extra for sprinkling

1 tsp coffee extract
75 g/2¾ oz plain flour, sifted
30 g finely chopped walnuts
roughly chopped walnuts,
  to decorate

### filling
175 ml/6 fl oz double cream
40 g/1½ oz icing sugar, plus
  extra, sifted, for dusting
1 tbsp coffee liqueur

> 1 Preheat the oven to 200°C/400°F/Gas Mark 6. Grease a 33 x 22 cm-/13 x 8½-inch Swiss roll tin and line with non-stick baking parchment.

> 2 Place the eggs, egg white and sugar in a bowl over a pan of very hot water. Whisk with an electric whisk until pale and thick enough to leave a trail.

> 3 Whisk in the coffee extract, then fold in the flour and walnuts lightly with a metal spoon.

> 4 Spoon into the tin, spreading evenly. Bake in the preheated oven for 12–15 minutes, until golden brown and firm.

**>5** Sprinkle a sheet of baking parchment with caster sugar. Turn out the roulade onto the paper and peel off the lining paper. Trim the edges.

**>6** Quickly roll up the sponge from one short side, with the paper inside. Cool completely.

**>7** For the filling, place the cream, sugar and liqueur in a bowl and whisk until the mixture begins to hold its shape.

**>8** Carefully unroll the roulade, remove the paper and spread the cream over. Roll up carefully.

Serve the roulade dusted with icing sugar, topped with roughly chopped walnuts.

# blueberry & passionfruit drizzle squares

**makes 9 squares**

**ingredients**
150 g/5½ oz butter, softened, plus extra for greasing
2 eggs

175 g/6 oz golden caster sugar
175 g/6 oz self-raising flour, sifted
90 ml/3 fl oz milk

finely grated zest of 1 lemon
225 g/8 oz blueberries

**syrup**
4 ripe passionfruit
115 g/4 oz icing sugar, plus extra, sifted, for dusting

> 1  Preheat the oven to 190°C/375°F/Gas Mark 5. Grease and base-line a 23-cm/9-inch square cake tin.

> 2  Whisk the butter, eggs and sugar until pale and fluffy. Fold in the flour lightly and evenly.

> 3  Stir in the milk, lemon zest and 175 g/6 oz blueberries. Spread into the cake tin.

> 4  Bake in the preheated oven for 25–30 minutes, until firm and golden brown. Remove from the oven and leave in the tin.

**>5** Meanwhile, make the syrup. Scoop the pulp from the passionfruit and rub through a sieve. Discard the pips.

**>6** Place the icing sugar and passionfruit juice in a saucepan and heat gently, stirring, until the sugar dissolves.

**>7** Prick the warm cake with a fork, and spoon the syrup evenly over the surface.

**>8** Leave the cake to cool completely in the tin then cut into 9 squares.

Top the squares with the reserved blueberries and dust with icing sugar before serving.

# apple streusel bars

**makes 14 bars**

### ingredients

125 g/4½ oz unsalted
  butter, softened,
  plus extra
  for greasing
2 crisp eating
  apples, peeled,
  cored and diced
2 tbsp lemon juice
125 g/4½ oz golden
  caster sugar
1 tsp vanilla extract
2 eggs, beaten
150 g/5½ oz self-
  raising flour

### topping

40 g/1½ oz blanched
  almonds, finely
  chopped
40 g/1½ oz plain flour
40 g/1½ oz light
  muscovado sugar
½ tsp ground
  cinnamon
30 g/1 oz unsalted
  butter, melted

> **>1** Preheat the oven to 180°C/350°F/Gas Mark 4. Grease and line a 28 x 18-cm/11 x 7-inch traybake tin. Sprinkle the apples with lemon juice.

> **>2** Cream together the butter, sugar and vanilla extract until pale. Gradually add the eggs, beating thoroughly.

Cut into bars and serve cold
or warm.

**>3** Sift over the flour and fold in evenly, then stir in the apples. Spread evenly in the tin.

**>4** For the topping, mix all the ingredients to a crumbly texture, sprinkle over the cake and bake in the preheated oven for 45–55 minutes, unti firm and golden.

# frosted carrot cake

**serves 16**

**ingredients**
175 ml/6 fl oz sunflower oil,
  plus extra for greasing
175 g/6 oz light muscovado
  sugar
3 eggs, beaten

175 g/6 oz grated carrots
85 g/3 oz sultanas
55 g/2 oz walnut pieces
grated rind of 1 orange
175 g/6 oz self-raising flour
1 tsp bicarbonate of soda

1 tsp ground cinnamon
½ tsp grated nutmeg
strips of orange zest,
  to decorate

**frosting**
200 g/7 oz cream cheese
100 g/3½ oz icing sugar
2 tsp orange juice

>1  Preheat the oven to 180°C/350°F/Gas Mark 4. Grease and line a 23-cm/9-inch square cake tin.

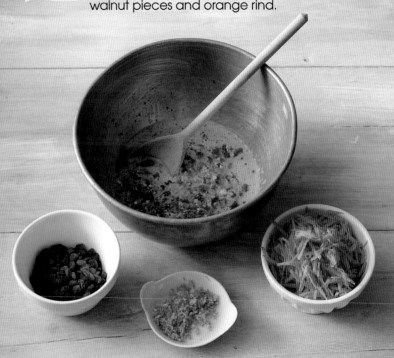

>2  In a large bowl beat together the oil, sugar and eggs. Stir in the grated carrots, sultanas, walnut pieces and orange rind.

>3  Sift the flour, bicarbonate of soda, cinnamon and nutmeg together into the bowl, then mix evenly into the carrot mixture.

>4  Spoon the mixture into the prepared cake tin and bake in the preheated oven for 40–45 minutes, until well risen and firm to the touch.

**>5** Cool in the tin for 5 minutes, then turn out
onto a wire rack to cool completely.

**>6** For the frosting, combine the cheese, icing sugar and
orange juice in a bowl and beat until smooth. Spread
over the top of the cake and swirl with a palette knife.

Decorate with strips of orange zest and serve cut into squares.

# chocolate chip brownies

**makes 12 brownies**

**ingredients**

225 g/8 oz butter, softened, plus extra for greasing
150 g/5½ oz plain chocolate, broken into pieces

225 g/8 oz self-raising flour
125 g/4½ oz caster sugar
4 eggs, beaten
75 g/2¾ oz pistachio nuts, chopped

100 g/3½ oz white chocolate, roughly chopped
icing sugar, sifted, for dusting

>**1** Preheat the oven to 180°C/350°F/Gas Mark 4. Grease and line a 23-cm/9-inch square baking tin.

>**2** Place the plain chocolate and the butter in a heatproof bowl set over a saucepan of simmering water. Stir until melted, then leave to cool slightly.

>**3** Sift the flour into a separate bowl and stir in the caster sugar.

>**4** Stir the eggs into the chocolate mixture, then pour into the flour and sugar and beat well.

>5 Stir in the nuts and white chocolate.

>6 Pour the mixture into the prepared tin, using a palette knife to spread evenly.

>7 Bake in the preheated oven for 30–35 minutes, or until firm to the touch around the edges. Cool in the tin for 20 minutes, then turn out onto a wire rack to cool completely.

>8 Dust with icing sugar and leave to cool completely.

Cut into 12 squares and serve.

# cinnamon squares

**makes 16 squares**

### ingredients

225 g/8 oz butter,
  softened, plus
  extra for greasing
225 g/8 oz caster
  sugar
3 eggs, lightly beaten
225 g/8 oz self-raising
  flour
½ tsp bicarbonate of
  soda
1 tbsp ground cinnamon
150 ml/5 fl oz soured
  cream
55 g/2 oz sunflower
  seeds

> **1** Preheat the oven to 180°C/350°F/Gas Mark 4.
> Grease and line a 23-cm/9-inch square cake tin.

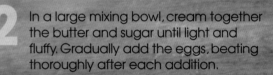

> **2** In a large mixing bowl, cream together
> the butter and sugar until light and
> fluffy. Gradually add the eggs, beating
> thoroughly after each addition.

Cut into 16 squares and serve.

**>3** Sift the flour, bicarbonate of soda and cinnamon into the creamed mixture and fold in with a metal spoon. Mix in the soured cream and sunflower seeds until well combined. Spoon into the prepared tin and smooth the surface with the back of a spoon.

**>4** Bake in the preheated oven for about 45 minutes, until firm to the touch. Loosen the edges and turn out onto a wire rack to cool completely.

# pastries

>4

>5

>6

# cinnamon swirls

**makes 12 swirls**

### ingredients

25 g/1 oz butter, cut into small
  pieces, plus extra for greasing
225 g/8 oz strong white flour
½ tsp salt

7 g/¼ oz easy-blend dried
  yeast
1 egg, lightly beaten
125 ml/4 fl oz lukewarm milk
2 tbsp maple syrup, for glazing

### filling

55 g/2 oz butter, softened
2 tsp ground cinnamon
50 g/1¾ oz soft light brown sugar
50 g/1¾ oz currants

**>1** Grease a baking sheet and a bowl. Sift the flour and salt into a mixing bowl and stir in the yeast.

**>2** Rub in the chopped butter with your fingertips until the mixture resembles breadcrumbs. Add the egg and milk and mix to form a dough.

**>3** Form the dough into a ball, place in the greased bowl, cover and leave to stand in a warm place for about 40 minutes, or until doubled in volume.

**>4** Punch down the dough lightly for 1 minute, then roll out to a rectangle measuring 30 x 23 cm/12 x 19 inches.

**>5** For the filling, cream together the softened butter, cinnamon and sugar until light and fluffy.

**>6** Spread the filling over the dough, leaving a 2.5-cm/1-inch border. Sprinkle the currants evenly over the top. Roll up the dough from one of the long edges and press down to seal.

**>7** Preheat the oven to 190°C/375°F/Gas Mark 5. Cut the roll into 12 slices and place them, cut side down, on the prepared baking sheet. Cover and leave to stand for 30 minutes.

**>8** Bake in the preheated oven for 20–30 minutes, or until the swirls are well risen.

Brush with maple syrup and leave to
cool slightly before serving.

# strawberry éclairs

makes 16–18 éclairs

## ingredients

### pastry
55 g/2 oz unsalted butter,
    plus extra for greasing
150 ml/5 fl oz water
8 tbsp plain flour, sifted
2 eggs, beaten

### filling
200 g/7 oz strawberries
2 tbsp icing sugar
140 g/5 oz mascarpone cheese

>1 Preheat the oven to 220°C/425°F/Gas Mark 7. Grease 2 baking sheets. Heat the butter and water in a pan until boiling.

>2 Remove from the heat, quickly tip in the flour and beat until smooth. Transfer to a bowl.

>3 Gradually beat in the eggs with an electric hand mixer, until glossy.

>4 Spoon into a piping bag with a large plain nozzle and pipe up to eighteen 9-cm/3½-inch fingers on the baking sheets.

**>5** Bake in the preheated oven for 12–15 minutes, until golden brown. Cut a slit down the side of each éclair to release steam. Bake for a further 2 minutes. Cool on a wire rack.

**>6** Purée half the strawberries with the icing sugar.

**>7** Finely chop the remaining strawberries and stir into the mascarpone.

**>8** Pipe or spoon the mascarpone mixture into the éclairs.

Serve the éclairs with the strawberry purée spooned over. The éclairs are best served within an hour of filling.

# chocolate filo parcels

**makes 18 parcels**

### ingredients

55–85 g/2–3 oz butter, melted,
  plus extra for greasing
85 g/3 oz ground hazelnuts
1 tbsp finely chopped fresh
  mint
125 ml/4 fl oz soured cream
2 eating apples, peeled and
  grated
55 g/2 oz plain chocolate,
  melted
9 sheets filo pastry, about
  15 cm/6 inches square
icing sugar, sifted, for dusting

> **1** Preheat the oven to 190°C/375°F/Gas Mark 5.
> Grease a baking sheet. Mix the nuts, mint and
> soured cream in a bowl. Add the apples, stir in
> the chocolate and mix well.

> **2** Cut each pastry sheet into 4 squares.
> Brush 1 square with butter, then place
> a second square on top and brush
> with butter.

Dust with icing sugar
and serve.

>3 Place a tablespoonful of the chocolate mixture in the centre, bring up the corners and twist together. Repeat until all of the pastry and filling has been used.

>4 Place the parcels on the prepared baking sheet and bake in the preheated oven for about 10 minutes, until crisp and golden. Remove from the oven and leave to cool slightly.

# apple danish

**makes 12–16 pastries**

## ingredients

275 g/9¾ oz strong white flour,
  plus extra, sifted, for dusting
175 g/6 oz butter, well chilled,
  plus extra for greasing

½ tsp salt
7 g/¼ oz easy-blend dried
  yeast
2 tbsp caster sugar, plus extra
  for sprinkling

1 egg
1 tsp vanilla extract
6 tbsp lukewarm water
milk, for glazing

## filling

2 cooking apples, peeled,
  cored and chopped
grated rind of 1 lemon
3 tbsp sugar

> 1 Place the flour in a bowl and rub in 25 g/1 oz of the butter. Set aside. Dust the remaining butter with flour, grate coarsely into a bowl and chill. Stir the salt, yeast and sugar into the flour mixture.

> 2 In another bowl, beat the egg with the vanilla extract and water, add to the flour mixture and mix to form a dough. Knead for 10 minutes on a floured surface, then chill for 10 minutes.

> 3 Roll out the dough to a 30 x 20-cm/12 x 8-inch rectangle. Mark widthways into thirds and fold. Press the edges with a rolling pin and roll out to the same size as the original rectangle.

> 4 Sprinkle the grated butter evenly over the top two-thirds. Fold up the bottom third and fold down the top third. Press the edges, wrap in clingfilm and chill for 30 minutes. Repeat four times, chilling well each time. Chill overnight.

**>5** Mix together the filling ingredients. Preheat the oven to 200°C/400°F/Gas Mark 6. Grease two baking sheets.

**>6** Roll out the dough into a 40-cm/16-inch square and cut up to 16 squares. Pile some filling in the centre of each, reserving any juice. Brush the edges of the squares with milk and bring the corners together in the centre.

**>7** Place on the prepared baking sheets and chill for 15 minutes. Brush with the reserved juice and sprinkle with caster sugar.

**>8** Bake in the preheated oven for 10 minutes, reduce the temperature to 180°C/350°F/Gas Mark 4 and bake for a further 10–15 minutes, until browned.

Gently remove from the baking sheets
and serve.

# date, pistachio nut and honey slices

makes 12 slices

## ingredients

250 g/9 oz stoned dates, chopped
2 tbsp lemon juice
2 tbsp water

85 g/3 oz pistachio nuts, chopped
2 tbsp clear honey
milk, for glazing

## pastry

225 g/ 8 oz plain flour, sifted
25 g/1 oz golden caster sugar
150 g/5½ oz butter
4–5 tbsp cold water, to mix

**>1** Place the dates, lemon juice and water in a pan and bring to the boil, stirring. Remove from the heat.

**>2** Stir in the pistachio nuts and 1 tbsp honey, cover and leave to cool.

**>3** Preheat the oven to 200°C/400°F/Gas Mark 6. For the pastry, place the flour, sugar and butter in a food processor and process until the mixture resembles fine breadcrumbs.

**>4** Mix in just enough cold water to bind to a soft, not sticky, dough.

**5** Roll out the pastry on a floured surface to two 30 x 20-cm/12 x 8-inch rectangles. Place one on a baking sheet.

 **6** Spread the date and nut mixture to within 1 cm/½ inch of the edge. Top with the remaining pastry.

**7** Press to seal, trim the edges and mark into 12 slices. Glaze with milk.

**8** Bake in the preheated oven for 20–25 minutes, until golden. Brush with the remaining honey and cool on a wire rack.

Cut into slices and serve as a lunchbox snack.

# chocolate nut strudel

serves 6

### ingredients

150 g/5 ½ oz unsalted
   butter, melted, plus extra
   for greasing
200 g/7 oz mixed
   chopped nuts
115 g/4 oz plain
   chocolate, chopped
115 g/4 oz milk
   chocolate, chopped
115 g/4 oz white
   chocolate, chopped
200 g/7 oz filo pastry
3 tbsp golden syrup
55 g/2 oz icing sugar, sifted,
   for dusting

 **>1** Preheat the oven to 190°C/375°F/Gas Mark 5.
Lightly grease a baking sheet. Reserving a
tablespoonful, place the nuts in a bowl and
mix with the chocolate.

**>2** Place a sheet of pastry on a clean
tea towel. Brush with butter, drizzle
with golden syrup and sprinkle with
the nut and chocolate mixture. Place
another sheet on top and repeat the
procedure until you have used all
the nuts and chocolate.

Dust the strudel with icing sugar, slice and serve.

**>3** Use the tea towel to carefully roll up the strudel, place on the prepared baking sheet, drizzle with the remaining golden syrup and sprinkle with the reserved nuts.

**>4** Bake in the preheated oven for 20–25 minutes. If the nuts start to brown too much, cover the strudel with a sheet of foil.

# spiced pear & sultana strudel

serves 6

**ingredients**

85 g/3 oz unsalted butter, melted, plus extra for greasing
3 firm ripe pears, peeled, cored and diced

finely grated rind and juice of ½ lemon
75 g/2¾ oz demerara sugar
1 tsp ground allspice
55 g/2 oz sultanas

55 g/2 oz ground almonds

6 sheets filo pastry (half a 250 g/9 oz pack)
icing sugar, sifted, for dusting

> **1** Preheat the oven to 200°C/400°F/Gas Mark 6 and grease a baking sheet with butter.

> **2** Mix together the pears, lemon rind and juice, sugar, allspice, sultanas and half the almonds.

> **3** Place 2 sheets of filo pastry, slightly overlapping, on a clean tea towel.

> **4** Brush lightly with melted butter and sprinkle with a third of the almonds. Top with two more sheets, butter and almonds. Repeat once more.

**5** Spread the pear mixture down one long side, to within 2.5 cm/1 inch of the edge.

**6** Roll the pastry over to enclose the filling and roll up, using the tea towel to lift. Tuck the ends under.

**7** Brush with a little melted butter and bake in the preheated oven for 20–25 minutes, until golden and crisp.

**8** Lightly dust the strudel with icing sugar.

Serve the strudel warm or cold, cut into thick slices.

# baklava

serves 16

**ingredients**

225 g/8 oz walnut halves, finely
   chopped
225 g/8 oz shelled pistachio
   nuts, finely chopped
100 g/3½ oz blanched
   almonds, finely chopped

4 tbsp pine nuts, finely
   chopped
finely grated rind of 2 large
   oranges
6 tbsp sesame seeds
1 tbsp sugar
½ tsp ground cinnamon

½ tsp mixed spice
250 g/9 oz butter, melted, plus
   extra for greasing
23 sheets filo pastry

**syrup**
450 g/1 lb caster sugar

450 ml/16 fl oz water
5 tbsp honey
3 cloves

>1 Put the walnuts, pistachios, almonds and pine nuts in a bowl and stir in the orange rind, sesame seeds, sugar, cinnamon and mixed spice.

>2 Preheat the oven to 160°C/325°F/Gas Mark 3. Grease a 25-cm/10-inch square ovenproof dish, about 5 cm/2 inches deep.

>3 Stack the pastry sheets. Cut them to the size of the dish, using a ruler.

>4 Place a sheet of pastry on the base of the dish and brush with melted butter. Top with seven more sheets, brushing with butter between each layer.

> **5** Sprinkle with a generous 150 g/5½ oz of the filling. Top with three sheets of pastry, brushing each one with butter. Continue until you have used all the pastry and filling, ending with a top layer of three sheets.

> **6** Brush with butter. Cut into 5-cm/2-inch squares. Brush again with butter. Bake in the preheated oven for 1 hour.

> **7** Meanwhile, put all the syrup ingredients in a saucepan. Slowly bring to the boil, stirring to dissolve the sugar, then simmer for 15 minutes, without stirring, until a thin syrup forms. Leave to cool.

> **8** Remove the baklava from the oven and strain the syrup over the top. Leave to cool in the dish.

Cut into squares and serve.

# summer
# fruit tartlets

makes 12 tartlets

## ingredients

200 g/7 oz plain flour, plus
  extra for dusting
85 g/3 oz icing sugar, sifted
55 g/2 oz ground almonds
115 g/4 oz butter
1 egg yolk
1 tbsp milk

## filling

225 g/8 oz cream cheese
icing sugar, to taste, plus
  extra, sifted, for dusting
350 g/12 oz fresh summer
  berries

> **1**
Sift the flour and icing sugar into a bowl.
Stir in the almonds. Add the butter, rubbing
in until the mixture resembles breadcrumbs.
Add the egg yolk and milk and work in until
the dough binds together. Wrap in clingfilm
and chill for 30 minutes.

> **2**
Preheat the oven to 200°C/400°F/
Gas Mark 6. Roll out the dough on
a lightly floured surface and use it
to line 12 deep tartlet tins. Prick the
bases and press a piece of foil into
each.

Dust with sifted icing sugar and
serve immediately.

**>3** Bake in the preheated oven for
10–15 minutes, or until light golden
brown. Remove the foil and bake for
a further 2–3 minutes. Transfer to a wire
rack to cool.

**>4** Halve the strawberries. For the filling, place
the cream cheese and icing sugar in a bowl
and mix together. Place a spoonful of filling in
each tartlet and arrange the berries on top.

# apple pie

serves 6–8

**ingredients**
175 g/6 oz plain flour
pinch of salt
85 g/3 oz butter, cut into pieces

85 g/3 oz lard, cut into small
  pieces
about 1–2 tbsp water
beaten egg or milk, for glazing

**filling**
750 g–1 kg/1 lb 10 oz–2 lb 4 oz
  cooking apples, peeled,
  cored and sliced

125 g/4½ oz soft light brown
  sugar, plus extra for sprinkling
½–1 tsp ground cinnamon
about 1–2 tbsp water

> **1** Sift the flour and salt into a mixing bowl. Add the butter and lard, and rub in with your fingertips until the mixture resembles fine breadcrumbs.

> **2** Add enough cold water to mix to a firm dough. Wrap in clingfilm and chill for 30 minutes.

> **3** Preheat the oven to 220°C/425°F/Gas Mark 7. Thinly roll out almost two thirds of the pastry and use to line a deep 23-cm/9-inch pie plate.

> **4** For the filling, mix the apples with the sugar and cinnamon, and pack into the pastry case.

**5** Roll out the remaining pastry to form a lid. Dampen the edges of the pie rim with water and position the lid, pressing the edges firmly together. Trim and crimp the edges.

 **6** Use the pastry trimmings to cut out leaves or other shapes. Dampen and attach to the top of the pie.

 **7** Glaze the pie with beaten egg or milk, make one or two slits in the top and place the pie on a baking sheet.

 **8** Bake in the preheated oven for 20 minutes, then reduce the temperature to 180°C/350°F/ Gas Mark 4 and bake for a further 30 minutes, or until the pastry is a light golden brown.

Sprinkle with sugar and serve hot or cold.

# lemon meringue pie

**serves 6–8**

## ingredients

150 g/5½ oz plain flour, plus
   extra for dusting
85 g/3 oz butter, cut into small
   pieces, plus extra for greasing

35 g/1¼ oz icing sugar, sifted
finely grated rind of ½ lemon
½ egg yolk, beaten
1½ tbsp milk

**filling**

3 tbsp cornflour
300 ml/10 fl oz water
juice and grated rind of
   2 lemons

175 g/6 oz caster sugar
2 eggs, separated

**>1** Sift the flour into a bowl. Rub in the butter with your fingertips until the mixture resembles fine breadcrumbs. Mix in the icing sugar, lemon rind, egg yolk and milk.

**>2** Knead briefly on a lightly floured work surface. Wrap in clingfilm and chill in the refrigerator for 30 minutes.

**>3** Preheat the oven to 180°C/350°F/Gas Mark 4. Grease a 20-cm/8-inch round tart tin. Roll out the pastry to 5 mm/¼ inch thick, then use it to line the tin.

**>4** Prick all over with a fork, line with baking paper and fill with baking beans. Bake in the preheated oven for 15 minutes.

>5 Remove the pastry case from the oven and take out the paper and beans. Reduce the temperature to 150°C/300°F/Gas Mark 2.

>6 For the filling, mix the cornflour with a little water to form a paste. Put the remaining water in a saucepan. Stir the lemon juice and rind into the cornflour paste. Bring to the boil, stirring. Cook for 2 minutes. Cool slightly.

>7 Stir in 5 tablespoons of the caster sugar and the egg yolks, and pour into the pastry case.

>8 Whisk the egg whites in a clean, grease-free bowl until stiff. Gradually whisk in the remaining caster sugar and spread over the pie. Place on a baking sheet and bake for 40 minutes. Remove from the oven and cool.

Serve plain or decorate with whipped cream and fresh fruit.

# cherry & cinnamon tartlets

*makes 4 tartlets*

### ingredients

125 g/4½ oz plain flour, sifted
2 tbsp icing sugar, sifted
½ tsp ground cinnamon
70 g/2½ oz unsalted butter, at
   room temperature
1 egg yolk
2 tbsp cold water

### filling

350 g/12 oz cherries, pitted
150 ml/5 fl oz Greek-style yogurt
2 tbsp clear honey
cinnamon and whole cherries,
   to decorate

> **1** Preheat the oven to 190°C/375°F/Gas Mark 5.
> Place the flour, icing sugar, cinnamon and
> butter in a food processor and process until
> evenly blended.

> **2** Add the egg yolk and water to the
> mixture, and blend until it just binds to
> form a soft dough.

Drizzle the tartlets with honey, sprinkle with cinnamon and serve with whole cherries.

**>3** Divide the pastry into four and press into 4 x 18-cm/4-inch loose-based tartlet tins, pressing with your knuckles to spread evenly.

**>4** Place on a baking sheet and bake the tartlets blind for 12–15 minutes (see page 98), then remove from the oven and leave to cool. Stir the cherries into the yogurt and spoon into the cases.

# broccoli, pancetta & blue cheese galette

**serves 4**

**ingredients**

1 sheet ready-rolled puff pastry
  (half a pack)
225 g/8 oz small broccoli florets,
  halved if necessary
125 g/4½ oz diced pancetta

1 small red onion, sliced
100 g/3½ oz Gorgonzola or
  Roquefort cheese, chopped
ground black pepper
toasted pine nuts, to garnish

>1 Preheat the oven to 200°C/400°C/Gas Mark 6. Place the pastry on a baking sheet and lightly score a line all around, cutting only halfway through, to within 1 cm/½ inch of the edge.

>2 Steam or boil the broccoli for 4–5 minutes, until just tender. Drain.

>3 Fry the pancetta with the onion, stirring, until golden. Stir in the broccoli and season with black pepper.

>4 Spread the filling over the pastry, leaving the border clear.

>5 Scatter the pieces of cheese evenly over the top.

>6 Bake in the preheated oven for 25–30 minutes, until the pastry is risen and golden.

Sprinkle with toasted pine nuts and serve warm.

# tomato tarte tatin

**serves 4**

**ingredients**
25 g/1 oz butter
1 tbsp caster sugar
500 g/1 lb 2 oz cherry
  tomatoes, halved
1 clove garlic, crushed

2 tsp white wine vinegar
salt and pepper

**pastry**
250 g/9 oz plain flour, sifted
pinch of salt

140 g/5 oz butter
1 tbsp chopped oregano,
  plus extra to garnish
5-6 tbsp cold water

> **1** Preheat the oven to 200°C/400°F/ Gas Mark 6. Melt the butter in a heavy-based pan.

> **2** Add the sugar and stir over a fairly high heat until just turning golden brown.

> **3** Remove from the heat and quickly add the tomatoes, garlic and white wine vinegar, stirring to coat evenly. Season with salt and pepper.

> **4** Tip the tomatoes into a 23-cm/9-inch cake tin, spreading evenly.

**>5** For the pastry, place the flour, salt, butter and oregano in a food processor and process until the mixture resembles fine breadcrumbs.

**>6** Add just enough water to bind to a soft, but not sticky, dough.

**>7** Roll out the pastry to a 25-cm/10-inch round and place over the tomatoes, tucking in the edges. Pierce with a fork to let out steam.

**>8** Bake in the preheated oven for 25–30 minutes, until firm and golden. Rest for 2–3 minutes, then run a knife around the edge and turn out onto a warmed serving plate.

Sprinkle the tarte tatin with chopped oregano, and serve warm.

# asparagus prosciutto wraps

**makes 6 wraps**

### ingredients

225 g/8 oz asparagus, trimmed
375 g/13 oz pack ready rolled chilled puff pastry sheet
2 tbsp pesto
6 thin slices prosciutto
85 g/3 oz grated Emmental cheese
milk, for glazing
ground black pepper

>1 Preheat the oven to 220°C/425°F/Gas Mark 7. Cook the asparagus in boiling water for 5–6 minutes, until tender. Drain.

>2 Cut the pastry into 6 squares. Place on a baking sheet and spread 1 tsp pesto on the centre of each.

Serve the wraps warm or cold, as a lunchtime snack or picnic treat.

> **3** Divide the asparagus into six bunches and wrap each in a prosciutto slice. Place diagonally on each square and top with grated cheese and pepper.

> **4** Lift opposite corners over to meet on top, brushing with milk to glaze. Bake in the preheated oven for 15–20 minutes, until golden.

119

# small cakes & biscuits

>4

>5

>6

# frosted peanut butter cupcakes

**makes 16 cupcakes**

### ingredients
55 g/2 oz butter, softened
225 g/8 oz soft light brown
 sugar
115 g/4 oz crunchy peanut
 butter

2 eggs, lightly beaten
1 tsp vanilla extract
225 g/8 oz plain white flour
2 tsp baking powder
100 ml/3½ fl oz milk

### frosting
200 g/7 oz cream cheese
25 g/1 oz butter, softened
225 g/8 oz icing sugar

> **1** Preheat the oven to 180°C/350°F/Gas Mark 4. Put 16 double-layer paper cases on a baking sheet.

> **2** Put the butter, sugar and peanut butter in a bowl and beat together until well mixed. Gradually add the eggs, beating well after each addition, then add the vanilla extract.

> **3** Sift in the flour and baking powder into a bowl, then use a metal spoon to fold in, alternating with the milk.

> **4** Spoon the mixture into the paper cases and bake in the preheated oven for 25 minutes, or until well risen and golden brown. Transfer to a wire rack and leave to cool.

**>5** For the frosting, put the cream cheese and butter into a large bowl and beat together until smooth. Sift in the icing sugar, then beat until well mixed.

**>6** When the cupcakes are cold, spread some frosting on top of each, swirling with a round-bladed knife.

# chocolate butterfly cupcakes

**makes 12 cupcakes**

### ingredients

125 g/4½ oz soft margarine
125 g/4½ oz caster sugar
150 g/5½ oz self-raising flour,
  sifted

2 large eggs
2 tbsp cocoa powder
25 g/1 oz plain chocolate,
  melted

**lemon buttercream**
100 g/3½ oz unsalted butter,
  softened
225 g/8 oz icing sugar, sifted,
  plus extra for dusting

grated rind of ½ lemon
1 tbsp lemon juice

> **1** Preheat the oven to 180°C/350°F/Gas Mark 4. Place 12 paper cases in a shallow bun tin.

> **2** Place the margarine, caster sugar, flour, eggs and cocoa powder in a large bowl, and beat until the mixture is just smooth. Beat in the melted chocolate.

> **3** Spoon the mixture into the paper cases, filling them three-quarters full.

> **4** Bake in the preheated oven for 15 minutes, or until well risen. Transfer to a wire rack and leave to cool completely.

**>5** For the buttercream, place the butter in a mixing bowl and beat until fluffy. Gradually add in the icing sugar, lemon rind and lemon juice, beating well with each addition.

**>6** Cut the top off each cake, using a serrated knife. Cut each cake top in half. Spread the lemon buttercream over the cut surface of each cake and push the two pieces of cake top into the icing to form wings.

Dust with icing sugar.

# fairy cupcakes

**makes 16 cupcakes**

### ingredients
115 g/4 oz unsalted butter
115 g/4 oz caster sugar
2 eggs, beaten
115 g/4 oz self-raising flour
sugar flowers, hundreds and
  thousands, glacé cherries
  and/or chocolate strands, to
  decorate

### icing
200 g/7 oz icing sugar
about 2 tbsp lukewarm water
few drops of food colouring
  (optional)

**>1** Preheat the oven to 180°C/350°F/Gas Mark 4. Put 16 double-layer paper cases on a baking sheet.

**>2** Place the butter and caster sugar in a large bowl and cream together until pale and fluffy. Gradually add the eggs, beating well after each addition. Fold in the flour, using a metal spoon.

Decorate the cupcakes with sugar flowers, hundreds and thousands and glacé cherries, and serve.

**>3** Spoon the mixture into the paper cases and bake in the preheated oven for 15–20 minutes, until well risen. Remove from the oven and place on a wire rack to cool.

**>4** For the icing, sift the icing sugar into a bowl and add enough water to mix to a smooth paste, thick enough to coat the back of a spoon. Stir in a few drops of food colouring, if using, then spread over the cakes.

# double ginger cupcakes

**makes about 12 cupcakes**

**ingredients**
175 g/6 oz plain flour
1 tbsp baking powder
2 tsp ground ginger
175 g/6 oz unsalted butter,
  softened

175 g/6 oz light muscovado
  sugar
3 eggs, beaten
25 g/1 oz crystallized stem
  ginger, finely chopped

**frosting**
200 g/7 oz ricotta cheese
85 g/3 oz icing sugar, sifted
finely grated rind 1 tangerine
diced crystallized ginger,
  to decorate

**>1** Preheat the oven to 190°C/375°F/Gas Mark 5. Place 12 paper cases in a shallow bun tin.

**>2** Sift the flour, baking powder and ground ginger into a large bowl.

**>3** Add the butter, muscovado sugar and eggs and beat well until smooth. Stir in the crystallized ginger.

**>4** Spoon the mixture into the paper cases. Bake in the preheated oven for 15–20 minutes, until well risen. Cool on a wire rack.

**>5** For the frosting, mix together the ricotta, icing sugar and tangerine rind until smooth.

**>6** Spoon a little frosting onto each cake and spread over the surface to cover.

Top the cupcakes with diced crystallized ginger and serve.

# low-fat blueberry muffins

**makes 12 muffins**

### ingredients

225 g/8 oz plain flour
1 tsp bicarbonate of soda
¼ tsp salt

1 tsp ground allspice
115 g/4 oz caster sugar
3 large egg whites
3 tbsp low-fat margarine

150 ml/5 fl oz thick low-fat
natural yogurt or blueberry-
flavoured yogurt

1 tsp vanilla extract
85 g/3 oz fresh blueberries

> 1

Preheat the oven to 190°C/375°F/Gas Mark 5.
Place 12 paper cases in a shallow bun tin.

> 2

Sift the flour, bicarbonate of soda, salt and
half the allspice into a large mixing bowl.
Add six tablespoons of the sugar and mix
together well.

> 3

In a separate bowl, whisk the egg whites
together. Add the margarine, yogurt and
vanilla extract and mix together well,
then stir in the blueberries
until thoroughly mixed.

> 4

Add the fruit mixture to the dry ingredients,
then gently stir until just combined. Do not
overstir – it is fine for it to be a little lumpy.

**5** Divide the mixture evenly between the paper cases to about two-thirds full. Mix the remaining sugar with the remaining allspice and sprinkle over the muffins.

**6** Bake in the preheated oven for 25 minutes, or until well risen. Remove the muffins from the oven.

Leave to cool or serve warm.

# lemon poppy
# seed madeleines

**makes about 30 madeleines**

## ingredients
oil, for greasing
3 eggs
1 egg yolk
finely grated rind of
  1 lemon
140 g/5 oz golden caster
  sugar
140 g/5 oz plain flour
1 tsp baking powder
140 g/5 oz unsalted
  butter, melted and
  cooled
1 tbsp poppy seeds

**>1** Preheat the oven to 190°C/375°F/Gas Mark 5.
Lightly grease three 12-hole madeleine tins.

**>2** Whisk the eggs, yolk, lemon rind and
sugar in a large bowl until very pale
and thick.

Turn out the cakes and cool on a wire rack, then serve very fresh.

>3 Sift the flour and baking powder over the mixture and fold in lightly using a metal spoon. Fold in the melted butter and poppy seeds.

>4 Spoon into the tins and bake in the preheated oven for about 10 minutes, until well risen.

# apricot, macadamia & white chocolate chunk muffins

**makes 12 muffins**

### ingredients
280 g/10 oz plain flour
1 tbsp baking powder
115 g/ 4 oz golden caster sugar
85 g/3 oz ready to eat dried
   apricots, chopped
55 g/2 oz macadamia nuts,
   chopped
55 g/2 oz white chocolate,
   chopped
2 eggs, beaten
200 ml/7 fl oz buttermilk
100 ml/31/2 fl oz sunflower oil

**>1** Preheat the oven to 200°C/400°F/Gas Mark 6.
Place 12 paper muffin cases in a muffin tray
or on a baking sheet.

**>2** Sift the flour and baking powder into
a bowl and stir in the sugar, apricots,
nuts and chocolate.

Serve the muffins warm, preferably on the day of making.

**>3** Beat together the eggs, buttermilk and oil, then add to the bowl and stir to mix evenly.

**>4** Spoon the mixture into the muffin cases and bake in the preheated oven for 20–25 minutes, until well risen.

# polenta berry crunch buns

**makes 18 buns**

**ingredients**

225 g/8 oz self-raising flour,
  sifted
85 g/3 oz polenta
150 g/5½ oz golden caster
  sugar

150 g/5½ oz unsalted butter
finely grated rind of 1 lemon
1 egg, beaten
2–3 tbsp lemon juice
150 g/5½ oz mixed berries

> 1   Preheat the oven to 200°C/400°F/Gas Mark 6. Place 18 paper cases in two shallow bun tins.

> 2   Place the flour, polenta, sugar and butter in a food processor and process to resemble fine breadcrumbs.

> 3   Stir the lemon rind into the mixture.

> 4   Stir in the egg with just enough lemon juice to make a soft, crumbly dough.

>5 Fold in the berries with a
metal spoon, mixing evenly.

>6 Spoon the mixture into the
cake cases and bake for about
20 minutes, until golden brown.
Cool the cakes on a wire rack.

The cakes can be stored for 2–3 days in an airtight container, or frozen for up to 1 month.

# classic oatmeal biscuits

**makes 10–20 biscuits**

### ingredients

175 g/6 oz butter or
margarine, plus extra for
greasing
275 g/9¾ oz demerara
sugar
1 egg
4 tbsp water
1 tsp vanilla extract
375 g/13 oz rolled oats
140 g/5 oz plain flour, sifted
1 tsp salt
½ tsp bicarbonate of soda

**>1** Preheat the oven to 350°F/180°C/Gas Mark 4
and grease a large baking sheet.

**>2** Cream the butter and sugar
together in a large mixing bowl.
Beat in the egg, water and vanilla
extract until the mixture is smooth.

For a sweeter option, drizzle with melted chocolate.

>3 In a separate bowl, mix the oats, flour, salt and bicarbonate of soda. Gradually stir the oat mixture into the creamed mixture until thoroughly combined.

>4 Place well-spaced tablespoonfuls of the mixture onto the prepared baking tray. Bake in the preheated oven for 15 minutes, or until golden brown. Remove from the oven and cool on a wire rack.

# marzipan whirls

**makes 8 whirls**

**ingredients**

125 g/4½ oz unsalted butter,
  softened
30 g/1 oz caster sugar

½ tsp almond essence
125 g/4½ oz plain flour, sieved
1 tbsp milk, to mix
40 g/1½ oz almond paste

4 tsp apricot jam, warmed
icing sugar, sifted, for dusting

**>1** Preheat the oven to 190°C/375°F/Gas Mark 5. Place 8 paper cases in a shallow bun tin.

**>2** Place the butter, caster sugar and almond essence in a food processor and process until pale and fluffy.

**>3** Add the flour and process to a soft dough, adding milk if necessary.

**>4** Spoon the mixture into a piping bag fitted with a large star vegetable nozzle.

**>5** Pipe the mixture in a spiral around the sides of each case, leaving a dip in the centre.

**>6** Cut the almond paste into 8 cubes and press one into the centre of each whirl.

**>7** Bake in the preheated oven for 15–20 minutes, until pale and golden. Lift the cakes onto a wire rack to cool.

**>8** Once the cakes have cooled, spoon a little of the apricot jam into the centre of each.

Dust the cakes with icing sugar, and serve.

# frosted cherry rings

**makes 15–18 rings**

**ingredients**

115 g/4 oz unsalted butter, plus
  extra for greasing
85 g/3 oz golden caster sugar

1 egg yolk
finely grated rind of ½ lemon
200 g/7 oz plain flour, plus extra
  for dusting

55 g/2 oz glacé cherries, finely
  chopped

**icing**

85 g/3 oz icing sugar, sifted
1½ tbsp lemon juice

> **1**  Preheat the oven to 200°C/400°F/Gas Mark 6. Lightly grease two baking trays.

> **2**  Cream together the butter and caster sugar until pale and fluffy. Beat in the egg yolk and lemon rind.

> **3**  Sift in the flour, stir, then add the glacé cherries, mixing with your hands to a soft dough.

> **4**  Roll out the dough on a lightly floured surface to about 5 mm/¼ inch thick. Stamp out 8-cm/3¼-inch rounds with a biscuit cutter.

**5** Stamp out the centre of each round with a 2.5-cm/1-inch cutter and place the rings on the prepared baking trays. Re-roll any trimmings and cut more biscuits.

**6** Bake in the preheated oven for 12–15 minutes, until firm and golden brown.

**7** Allow to cool on the baking trays for 2 minutes, then transfer to a wire rack to finish cooling.

**8** For the frosting, mix the icing sugar to a smooth paste with the lemon juice. Drizzle over the biscuits and leave until set.

Serve with tea or coffee as a
mid-morning treat.

# chocolate hazelnut flapjack cookies

**makes 16–18 cookies**

### ingredients
85 g/3 oz unsalted butter,
  plus extra for greasing
175 g/6 oz chocolate
  hazelnut spread
175 g/6 oz porridge oats
70 g/2½ oz blanched
  hazelnuts, chopped

>1 Preheat the oven to 200°C/400°F/Gas Mark 6. Grease a baking sheet.

>2 Place the butter and chocolate hazelnut spread in a pan and heat gently until just melted.

The cookies can be stored in an airtight container for up to 2 weeks.

>3 Add the porridge oats and hazlenuts to the chocolate mixture and stir to combine thoroughly.

>4 Shape the mixture into 16–18 equal-size balls, then press onto the prepared baking sheet. Bake in the preheated oven for 10–12 minutes, remove from the oven and leave until firm before transferring the cookies to a wire rack to finish cooling.

# cranberry & pine nut biscotti

**makes 18–20 biscotti**

**ingredients**

butter or oil, for greasing
85 g/3 oz light muscovado
  sugar

1 large egg
140 g/5 oz plain flour
½ tsp baking powder
1 tsp ground allspice

55 g/2 oz dried cranberries
55 g/2 oz pine nuts, toasted

1 Preheat the oven to 180°C/350°F/Gas Mark 4. Grease a baking sheet.

2 Whisk together the sugar and egg until pale and thick enough to form a trail.

3 Sift the flour, baking powder and allspice and fold into the mixture.

4 Stir in the cranberries and pine nuts and mix lightly to a smooth dough.

**>5** With lightly floured hands, shape the mixture into a long roll, about 28 cm/ 11 inch long. Press to flatten slightly.

**>6** Lift the dough onto the baking sheet and bake in the preheated oven for 20–25 minutes, until golden.

**>7** Cool for 3–4 minutes, then cut into 1.5-cm/ ⅝-inch thick slices and arrange on the baking sheet.

**>8** Bake in the oven for 10 minutes, or until golden. Remove from the oven, transfer to a wire rack and leave to cool.

When cool, store the biscotti in
an airtight tin for up to 2–3 weeks.

# mini florentines

**makes 20–30 florentines**

**ingredients**

75 g/2¾ oz butter
75 g/2¾ oz caster sugar
25 g/1 oz sultanas or raisins

25 g/1 oz glacé cherries,
   chopped
25 g/1 oz crystallized stem
   ginger, finely chopped

25 g/1 oz sunflower seeds
100 g/3½ oz flaked almonds
2 tbsp double cream

175 g/6 oz plain or milk
   chocolate, broken into pieces

**1** Preheat the oven to 180°C/350°F/ Gas Mark 4. Line two baking trays.

**2** Place the butter in a small saucepan and melt over a low heat. Add the sugar, stir until dissolved, then bring to the boil.

**3** Remove from the heat and stir in the sultanas, glacé cherries, crystallized ginger, sunflower seeds and almonds. Mix well, then beat in the cream.

**4** Place small, well-spaced teaspoons of mixture onto the prepared baking trays. Bake in the preheated oven for 10–12 minutes, or until light golden in colour.

**>5** Remove from the oven and, while still hot, use a circular biscuit cutter to pull in the edges to form perfect circles. Leave to cool and turn crisp before removing from the baking trays.

**>6** Put the chocolate in a heatproof bowl set over a saucepan of gently simmering water and stir until melted. Spread most of the chocolate onto a sheet of baking paper.

**>7** When the chocolate is on the point of setting, place the biscuits flat-side down on the chocolate and let it harden completely.

**>8** Cut around the florentines and remove from the baking paper. Spread the remaining chocolate on the coated side of the florentines, using a fork to mark waves. Leave to set.

Serve or present as a gift in a pretty box.

# chocolate chip cookies

**makes 8 cookies**

### ingredients

unsalted butter, melted,
  for greasing
175 g/6 oz plain flour, sifted
1 tsp baking powder
125 g/4½ oz margarine, melted
85 g/3 oz light muscovado
  sugar
55 g/2 oz caster sugar
½ tsp vanilla extract
1 egg
125 g/4½ oz plain chocolate
  chips

 **>1**   Preheat the oven to 190°C/375°F/Gas Mark 5.
Line and lightly grease two baking trays.

 **>2**   Place all of the ingredients in a large
mixing bowl and beat until well
combined.

Serve or store in an airtight box.

>3 Place well-spaced tablespoonfuls of the mixture onto the prepared baking trays.

>4 Bake in the preheated oven for 10–12 minutes, or until golden brown. Transfer to a wire rack and leave to cool.

169

# breads

>4

>5

>6

# crusty white bread

**makes 1 loaf**

**ingredients**

1 egg
1 egg yolk
150–200 ml/5–7 fl oz lukewarm
  water

500 g/1 lb 2 oz strong white
  flour, sifted, plus extra for
  dusting
1½ tsp salt
2 tsp sugar

1 tsp easy-blend dried yeast
25 g/1 oz butter, diced
oil, for greasing

**>1** Place the egg and egg yolk in a jug and beat lightly to mix. Add enough water to make up to 300 ml/10 fl oz. Stir well.

**>2** Place the flour, salt, sugar and yeast in a large bowl. Add the butter and rub it in with your fingertips until the mixture resembles fine breadcrumbs.

**>3** Make a well in the centre, add the egg mixture and work to a smooth dough. Turn out onto a lightly floured surface and knead well for about 10 minutes, until smooth.

**>4** Brush a bowl with oil. Shape the dough into a ball, place in the bowl, cover and leave to rise in a warm place for 1 hour, or until doubled in volume.

**>5** Preheat the oven to 220°C/425°F/Gas Mark 7. Oil a 900-g/2-lb loaf tin. Turn out the dough onto a lightly floured surface and knead for 1 minute until smooth.

**>6** Shape the dough so it is the same length as the loaf tin and three times the width. Fold the dough in three widthways and place it in the tin with the join underneath.

**>7** Cover and leave in a warm place for 30 minutes, until the dough has risen above the tin.

**>8** Place in the preheated oven and bake for 30 minutes, or until firm and golden brown. Transfer to a wire rack and leave to cool.

Cut into thick slices and serve.

# plaited poppy seed bread

**makes 1 loaf**

### ingredients

225 g/8 oz strong white flour,
  plus extra for dusting
1 tsp salt
2 tbsp skimmed milk powder
1½ tbsp caster sugar

1 tsp easy-blend dried yeast
175 ml/6 fl oz lukewarm water
2 tbsp vegetable oil, plus extra
  for greasing
5 tbsp poppy seeds

### topping

1 egg yolk
1 tbsp milk
1 tbsp caster sugar
2 tbsp poppy seeds

> **1** Sift the flour and salt together into a bowl and stir in the milk powder, sugar and yeast. Make a well in the centre, pour in the water and oil and stir until the dough begins to come together.

> **2** Add the poppy seeds and knead until fully combined and the dough leaves the side of the bowl. Turn out onto a lightly floured surface and knead well for about 10 minutes, until smooth and elastic.

> **3** Brush a bowl with oil. Shape the dough into a ball, put it in the bowl, cover and leave to rise in a warm place for 1 hour, or until doubled in volume.

> **4** Oil a baking sheet. Turn out the dough onto a lightly floured surface, knock back and knead for 1–2 minutes. Divide into 3 equal pieces and shape each into a rope 25–30 cm/ 10–12 inches long.

>5 Place the ropes side by side and press together at one end. Plait the dough, pinch the other end together and tuck underneath.

>6 Put the loaf on the prepared baking sheet, cover and leave to rise in a warm place for 30 minutes. Meanwhile, preheat the oven to 200°C/400°F/Gas Mark 6.

>7 For the topping, beat the egg yolk with the milk and sugar. Brush the egg glaze over the top of the loaf and sprinkle with the poppy seeds.

>8 Bake in the preheated oven for 30–35 minutes, until golden brown. Transfer to a wire rack and leave to cool.

Serve plain or toasted as a
lunchtime treat.

# pesto & olive soda bread

*makes 1 loaf*

### ingredients
olive oil, for greasing
250 g/9 oz plain flour
250 g/9 oz wholemeal flour
1 tsp bicarbonate of soda
½ tsp salt
3 tbsp pesto
300 ml/½ pint buttermilk
  (approx)
55 g/2 oz pitted green olives,
  roughly chopped
milk, for glazing

> **1** Preheat the oven to 200°C/400°F/Gas Mark 6 and line and grease a baking tray. Sift the flours, bicarbonate of soda and salt into a bowl, adding back any bran from the sieve.

> **2** Mix the pesto and buttermilk. Stir into the flour with the olives, mixing to a soft dough. Add more liquid if needed.

Serve the soda bread on the day of baking.

>3 Shape the dough into a 20-cm/8-inch round and place on the baking tray. Flatten slightly and cut a deep cross with a sharp knife.

>4 Brush with milk and bake in the preheated oven for 30–35 minutes, until golden brown. The loaf should sound hollow when tapped underneath.

181

# spring onion & parmesan cornbread

**serves 16**

## ingredients

oil, for greasing
140 g/5 oz fine cornmeal
140 g/5 oz plain flour
4 tsp baking powder

2 tsp celery salt
55 g/2 oz Parmesan cheese,
  grated
2 eggs, beaten
400 ml/14 fl oz milk

55 g/2 oz butter, melted
1 bunch spring onions,
  chopped
ground black pepper

**>1** Preheat the oven to 190°C/375°F/Gas Mark 5. Grease a 23-cm/9-inch square baking tin.

**>2** Sift the cornmeal, flour, baking powder, celery salt and pepper into a bowl and stir in 40 g/1½ oz of the Parmesan.

**>3** Beat together the eggs, milk and melted butter.

**>4** Add the egg mixture to the dry ingredients and stir well to mix evenly.

**>5** Stir in the chopped spring onions and spread the mixture evenly into the tin.

**>6** Sprinkle the remaining Parmesan over the mixture. Bake in the preheated oven for 30–35 minutes, or until firm and golden.

Cut the cornbread into squares and serve warm.

# rye bread

**makes 1 loaf**

**ingredients**

450 g/1 lb rye flour
225 g/8 oz strong white flour,
  plus extra for dusting

2 tsp salt
2 tsp soft light brown sugar
1½ tsp easy-blend dried yeast
425 ml/15 fl oz lukewarm water

2 tsp vegetable oil, plus extra
  for greasing
1 egg white

> 1 Sift the flours and salt together into a bowl. Add the sugar and yeast and stir to mix. Make a well in the centre and pour in the water and oil.

> 2 Stir until the dough begins to come together, then knead until it leaves the side of the bowl. Turn out onto a lightly floured surface and knead for 10 minutes, until elastic and smooth.

> 3 Brush a bowl with oil. Shape the dough into a ball, put it in the bowl, cover and leave to rise in a warm place for 2 hours, or until doubled in volume.

> 4 Oil a baking tray. Turn out the dough onto a lightly floured surface and knock back, then knead for 10 minutes.

**>5** Shape the dough into a ball, put it on the prepared baking tray and cover. Leave to rise in a warm place for a further 40 minutes, or until doubled in volume.

**>6** Meanwhile, preheat the oven to 190°C/ 375°F/Gas Mark 5. Beat the egg white with 1 tablespoon of water in a bowl.

**>7** Bake the loaf in the preheated oven for 20 minutes, then remove from the oven and brush the top with the egg white glaze. Return to the oven and bake for a further 20 minutes.

**>8** Brush the top of the loaf with the glaze again and return to the oven for a further 20–30 minutes, until the crust is a rich brown colour. Transfer to a wire rack to cool.

Serve with good quality butter or a topping of your choice.

# irish soda bread

**makes 1 loaf**

### ingredients

butter, melted, for greasing
450 g/1 lb plain flour, plus extra
  for dusting
1 tsp salt
1 tsp bicarbonate of soda
400 ml/14 fl oz buttermilk

**>1** Preheat the oven to 220°C/425°F/Gas Mark 7. Lightly grease a baking sheet.

**>2** Sift the dry ingredients into a mixing bowl. Make a well in the centre, pour in most of the buttermilk and mix well, using your hands. The dough should be very soft but not too wet. If necessary, add the remaining buttermilk.

Serve in slices with butter and a sweet or savoury topping.

> 3  Turn out the dough onto a floured surface and knead. Shape into a 20-cm/8-inch round.

> 4  Place the bread on the prepared baking sheet, cut a cross in the top and bake in the preheated oven for 25–30 minutes.

191

# pumpkin & seed twist

**makes 1 loaf**

**ingredients**

250 g/9 oz peeled pumpkin, diced
1 tsp fennel seeds

grated rind of 1 lemon
2 tbsp clear honey
500 g/1lb 2 oz strong plain flour
½ tsp salt

6 g sachet easy-blend dried yeast
300 ml/10 fl oz lukewarm water (approx)

oil, for greasing
milk, for glazing
2 tbsp pumpkin and sunflower seeds

> **1** Steam the pumpkin for 10 minutes or until tender. Drain thoroughly.

> **2** Mash the pumpkin and stir in the fennel seeds, lemon rind and honey.

> **3** Sift the flour and salt into a bowl and stir in the yeast. Add the pumpkin mixture.

> **4** Stir in enough water to make a soft dough and knead on a floured surface for 10 minutes, until smooth.

>5 Cover and leave in a warm place for 30 minutes or until doubled in volume. Shape the dough into two 35-cm/14-inch long ropes.

>6 Grease a baking tray. Twist the ropes together, pinching the ends. Cover and leave in a warm place for 1–1½ hours, until doubled in volume.

>7 Preheat the oven to 200°C/400°F/Gas Mark 6. Brush the loaf with milk and sprinkle with pumpkin and sunflower seeds.

>8 Bake in the preheated oven for 30–35 minutes, or until golden. It should sound hollow when tapped underneath. Cool on a wire rack.

Serve the loaf sliced with a hearty winter soup, or for an unusual breakfast.

195

# stromboli with salami, roasted peppers & cheese

**makes 1 loaf**

**ingredients**
500 g/1 lb 2 oz strong white
   flour, sifted
6 g sachet fast-action dried
   yeast
2 tsp sea salt flakes
3 tbsp olive oil, plus extra for
   brushing

350 ml/12 fl oz lukewarm water

**filling**
85 g/3 oz thinly sliced Italian
   salami
175 g/6 oz mozzarella cheese,
   chopped
25 g/1 oz basil leaves

2 red peppers, roasted,
   peeled, deseeded and sliced
   (or ready-roasted peppers
   from a jar)
freshly ground black pepper

> **1** Mix the flour, yeast and 1½ tsp salt, then stir in the oil with enough water to make a soft dough.

> **2** Knead the dough on a floured surface for about 10 minutes. Cover and leave in a warm place for 1 hour, or until doubled in volume.

> **3** Knead lightly for 2–3 minutes until smooth. Cover and leave for 10 minutes more.

> **4** Roll out the dough to a rectangle about 38 x 25-cm/15 x 10-inch in size, 1 cm/½ inch thick.

197

**>5** Preheat the oven to 200°C/400°F/Gas Mark 6. Spread the salami over the dough and top with the mozzarella, basil and peppers. Season with black pepper.

**>6** Grease a baking sheet. Roll the dough up firmly from the long side, pinch the ends and place on the baking sheet. Join underneath. Cover and leave for 10 minutes.

**>7** Pierce the roll deeply several times with a skewer.

**>8** Brush with oil and sprinkle with the remaining salt. Bake in the preheated oven for 30–35 minutes or until firm and golden. Cool on a wire rack.

Serve the bread fresh and warm, cut into thick slices.

# feta & olive scones

makes 8 scones

## ingredients

butter, for greasing
400 g/14 oz self-raising flour
¼ tsp salt
85 g/3 oz butter
40 g/1½ oz pitted black olives,
 chopped
40 g/1½ oz sun-dried tomatoes
 in oil, drained and chopped
85 g/3 oz feta cheese (drained
 weight), crumbled
200 ml/7 fl oz milk, plus extra
 for glazing
ground black pepper

> **1** Preheat the oven to 220°C/425°F/Gas Mark 7. Grease a baking sheet.

> **2** Sift the flour, salt and pepper into a bowl and rub in the butter evenly with your fingers.

Serve the scones fresh and warm, with extra butter if needed.

**>3** Stir in the olives, tomatoes and feta, then stir in just enough milk to make a soft, smooth dough.

**>4** Roll out on a floured surface to a 3-cm/1¼-inch thick rectangle. Cut into 6-cm/2½-inch squares. Place on the baking sheet, brush with milk and bake for 12–15 minutes, until golden.

# fresh croissants

**makes 6 croissants**

**ingredients**

500 g/1 lb 2 oz strong white
  flour sifted, plus extra
  for dusting
40 g/1½ oz caster sugar

1 tsp salt
2 tsp easy-blend dried yeast
300 ml/10 fl oz lukewarm milk
300 g/10½ oz butter, softened,
  plus extra for greasing

1 egg, lightly beaten with
1 tbsp milk, for glazing

> 1 Preheat the oven to 200°C/400°F/ Gas Mark 6. Mix the dry ingredients in a large bowl, make a well in the centre and add the milk. Mix to a soft dough, adding more milk if too dry.

> 2 Knead on a lightly floured work surface for 5–10 minutes, or until smooth and elastic. Place in a large greased bowl, cover and leave in a warm place until doubled in volume.

> 3 Meanwhile, place the butter between two sheets of baking paper and flatten with a rolling pin to form a 5-mm/¼-inch thick rectangle. Set aside in the refrigerator until required.

> 4 Knead the dough for 1 minute. Remove the butter from the refrigerator. Roll out the dough on a well-floured work surface to 45 x 15 cm/ 18 x 6 inches.

**>5** Place the butter in the centre of the dough, folding up the sides and squeezing the edges together gently. With the short end of the dough towards you, fold the top third down and the bottom third up.

**>6** Give the dough a quarter turn, roll out as big as the original rectangle and fold again. If the butter feels soft, wrap the dough in clingfilm and chill. Repeat the rolling process twice more.

**>7** Cut the dough in half and roll out each half into a 5-mm/¼-inch thick rectangle. Use a cardboard triangular template, base 18 cm/7 inches and sides 20 cm/8 inches, to cut out the croissants.

**>8** Brush the triangles with the glaze. Roll into croissant shapes, tucking the point underneath. Brush again with the glaze. Place on a baking sheet and leave to double in volume. Bake in the preheated oven for 15–20 minutes, until golden brown.

# cherry & peel spirals

**makes 8 spirals**

## ingredients

4 tbsp melted butter
100 g/3½ oz glacé cherries, chopped

40 g/1½ oz chopped mixed peel
55 g/2 oz soft light brown sugar
finely grated rind of 1 lemon
1 tsp ground allspice

250 g/9 oz strong plain flour
½ tsp salt
6 g sachet easy-blend dried yeast

125 ml/4 fl oz lukewarm milk, plus extra for glazing
1 egg, beaten

> **1** Grease a 20-cm/8-inch round cake tin with 1 tbsp butter. Mix together the cherries, peel, sugar, lemon rind and allspice.

> **2** Sift together the flour and salt, and stir in the yeast. Add the milk, egg and 2 tbsp butter and combine.

> **3** Knead to a smooth dough. Cover and leave in a warm place for 1–1½ hours or until doubled in volume.

> **4** Knead lightly, then roll out to a 25 x 30-cm/ 10 x 12-inch rectangle.

Brush with the remaining butter and sprinkle with the fruit mixture.

Roll up from the long side. Cut into 8 slices and arrange in the tin.

Cover and leave to rise in a warm place until doubled in volume. Preheat the oven to 190°C/375°F/Gas Mark 5.

Brush with milk and bake for 25–30 minutes, until firm and golden. Cool on a wire rack.

Gently pull the buns apart and serve.

# cinnamon spiced orange beignets

**makes 8 beignets**

### ingredients

250 g/9-oz plain flour
1 tsp easy-blend dried yeast
1½ tbsp caster sugar
125 ml/4 fl oz lukewarm milk
1 egg, beaten
finely grated rind of 1 small
  orange
1 tsp orange flower water
40 g/1½ oz butter, melted
sunflower oil, for deep frying
cinnamon sugar, for dusting
orange slices or segments,
  to serve

>1  Sift the flour into a bowl and stir in the yeast and sugar.

>2  Add the milk, egg, orange rind, flower water and butter and mix to a soft dough, kneading until smooth.

Sprinkle with cinnamon sugar and serve hot with orange slices or segments.

**>3** Cover and leave in a warm place until doubled in volume. Roll out on a lightly floured surface to 1 cm/½ inch in thickness, and cut into eight 7.5-cm/ 3-inch squares.

**>4** Heat the oil to 180°C/350°F. Fry the beignets in batches until golden brown. Remove with a slotted spoon and drain on kitchen paper.

211

# chocolate & saffron brioches

**makes 12 brioches**

**ingredients**

pinch of saffron strands
3 tbsp boiling water
55 g/2 oz butter, melted
250 g/9 oz strong plain flour

pinch of salt
1 tbsp caster sugar
6 g sachet easy-blend dried
 yeast
2 eggs, beaten

6 squares plain dark chocolate,
 halved (30 g/1 oz total)
milk, for glazing

**>1** Add the saffron to the boiling water and leave to cool completely.

**>2** Lightly brush 12 individual brioche tins or fluted bun tins with butter.

**>3** Sift the flour, salt and sugar and stir in the yeast. Add the saffron, saffron liquid, eggs and remaining butter to make a soft dough.

**>4** Knead until smooth, then cover and leave in a warm place for 1–1½ hours, or until doubled in volume.

213

> **5** Knead briefly then shape three-quarters of the dough into 12 balls. Place in the tins and press a piece of chocolate firmly into each.

> **6** Shape the remaining dough into 12 small balls with a pointed end. Brush with milk and press the balls in each bun, sealing well.

> **7** Cover with oiled polythene and leave in a warm place for 1½ hours, or until doubled in volume.

> **8** Preheat the oven to 200°C/400°F/Gas Mark 6. Brush with milk and bake in the preheated oven for 12–15 minutes, until firm and golden.

Turn out the brioches and serve warm – these are a perfect breakfast treat.

# crown loaf

serves 9

### ingredients
2 tbsp butter, diced, plus extra
  for greasing
225 g/8 oz strong white flour
½ tsp salt
7 g/¼ oz easy-blend dried
  yeast
125 ml/4 fl oz lukewarm milk
1 egg, lightly beaten

### filling
4 tbsp butter, softened
50 g/1¾ oz soft light brown
  sugar
2 tbsp chopped hazelnuts
1 tbsp crystallized ginger
50 g/1¾ oz chopped mixed
  peel
1 tbsp dark rum or brandy

### icing
115 g/4 oz icing sugar, sifted
1–2 tbsp lemon juice

> **1** Grease a baking tray. Sift the flour and salt into a bowl. Stir in the yeast. Rub in the diced butter with your fingertips. Add the milk and egg and mix to form a dough.

> **2** Place the dough in a greased bowl, cover and leave in a warm place for 40 minutes, or until doubled in volume.

> **3** Punch down lightly for 1 minute. Roll out to a 30 x 23-cm/12 x 9-inch rectangle.

> **4** For the filling, cream the butter and sugar until light and fluffy. Stir in the hazelnuts, ginger, mixed peel and rum.

**>5** Spread the filling over the dough, leaving a 2.5-cm/1-inch border.

**>6** Roll up the dough, starting from one of the long edges, into a sausage shape. Cut into slices at 5-cm/2-inch intervals and place in a circle on the prepared baking tray with the slices just touching.

**>7** Cover and leave in a warm place for 30 minutes. Meanwhile, preheat the oven to 190°C/375°F/Gas Mark 5. Bake the loaf in the preheated oven for 20–30 minutes, or until golden.

**>8** For the icing, mix the sugar with enough lemon juice to form a thin icing. Leave the loaf to cool slightly before drizzling with the icing. Allow the icing to set before serving.

Cut into 9 slices and serve.

# scones

**makes 9 scones**

### ingredients

450 g/1 lb plain flour, plus extra
   for dusting
½ tsp salt
2 tsp baking powder
55 g/2 oz butter
2 tbsp caster sugar
250 ml/9 fl oz milk, plus extra
   for glazing
strawberry jam and clotted
   cream, to serve

**>1** Preheat the oven to 220°C/425°F/Gas Mark 7. Sift the flour, salt and baking powder into a bowl. Rub in the butter using your fingertips until the mixture resembles fine breadcrumbs.

**>2** Stir in the sugar. Make a well in the centre and pour in the milk. Stir in using a palette knife and bring together to make a soft dough.

Serve freshly baked with strawberry jam and clotted cream.

>3 Turn out the dough onto a floured surface and very lightly flatten it until it is 1 cm/½ inch thick. Cut out scones using a 6-cm/2½-inch biscuit cutter and place on a lined baking sheet.

>4 Brush with a little milk and bake in the preheated oven for 10–12 minutes, until golden and well risen. Leave to cool on a wire rack.

# Index

allspice
  cherry & peel spirals 206–209
  cranberry & nut pine biscotti 160–163
  spiced pear & sultana strudel 90–93
almonds
  apple streusel bars 56–57
  baklava 94–97
  chocolate fudge cake 22–25
  classic cherry cake 18–21
  honey & almond cake 46–47
  marzipan whirls 150–153
  mini florentines 164–167
  rich almond cake 32–35
  spiced pear & sultana strudel 90–93
  summer fruit tartlets 98–99
apples
  apple danish 80–81
  apple pie 100–103
  apple streusel bars 56–57
  chocolate filo parcels 78–79
apricot, macadamia & white chocolate
    chunk muffins 142–143
asparagus prosciutto wraps 118–119

baklava 94–97
banana coconut loaf cake 28–31
basil: stromboli with salami, roasted
    peppers & cheese 196–199
berries
  polenta berry crunch buns 144–147
  summer fruit tartlets 98–99
  see also blueberries; cranberries;
    strawberries
biscuits & cookies
  chocolate chip cookies 168–169
  chocolate hazelnut flapjack
    cookies 158–159
  classic oatmeal biscuits 148–149
  cranberry & pine nut biscotti 160–163
  frosted cherry rings 154–157
  mini florentines 164–167
blueberries
  blueberry & passionfruit drizzle
    squares 52–55
  low-fat blueberry muffins 136–139
breads & yeast goods
  apple danish 80–81
  cherry & peel spirals 206–209
  chocolate & saffron brioches 212–215
  cinnamon spiced orange beignets 210–211

cinnamon swirls 70–73
crown loaf 216–219
crusty white bread 172–175
fresh croissants 202–205
irish soda bread 190–191
pesto & olive soda bread 180–181
plaited poppy seed bread 176–179
pumpkin & seed twist 192–195
rye bread 186–189
spring onion & parmesan
  cornbread 182–185
stromboli with salami, roasted peppers &
  cheese 196–199
broccoli, pancetta & blue cheese
  galette 110–113
brownies: chocolate chip brownies 62–65

cakes
  banana coconut loaf cake 28–31
  caramel peach gâteau 42–45
  chocolate fudge cake 22–25
  classic cherry cake 18–21
  coffee & walnut roulade 48–51
  double chocolate mint sponge 36–37
  frosted carrot cake 58–61
  honey & almond cake 46–47
  orange madeira ring 38–41
  rich almond cake 32–35
  victoria sponge cake 26–27
  see also small cakes and bars
caramel peach gateau 42–45
carrots: frosted carrot cake 58–61
cheese
  asparagus prosciutto wraps 118–119
  broccoli, pancetta & blue cheese
    galette 110–113
  feta & olive scones 200–201
  spring onion & parmesan
    cornbread 182–185
  stromboli with salami, roasted peppers &
    cheese 196–199
  see also cream cheese; ricotta cheese
cherries
  cherry & cinnamon tartlets 108–109
  cherry & peel spirals 206–209
  classic cherry cake 18–21
  frosted cherry rings 154–157
  mini florentines 164–167
chocolate
  apricot, macadamia & white chocolate

chunk muffins 142–143
  chocolate & saffron brioches 212–215
  chocolate butterfly cupcakes 126–129
  chocolate chip brownies 62–65
  chocolate chip cookies 168–169
  chocolate filo parcels 78–79
  chocolate fudge cake 22–25
  chocolate hazelnut flapjack
    cookies 158–159
  chocolate nut strudel 88–89
  double chocolate mint sponge 36–37
  mini florentines 164–167
cinnamon
  apple pie 100–103
  apple streusel bars 56–57
  baklava 94–97
  cherry & cinnamon tartlets 108–109
  cinnamon spiced orange beignets 210–211
  cinnamon squares 66–67
  cinnamon swirls 70–73
  frosted carrot cake 58–61
classic cherry cake 18–21
classic oatmeal biscuits 148–149
cloves: baklava 94–97
coconut: banana coconut loaf cake 28–31
coffee & walnut roulade 48–51
cranberry & pine nut biscotti 160–163
cream
  coffee & walnut roulade 48–51
  victoria sponge cake 26–27
  see also crème fraîche; soured cream
cream cheese
  frosted carrot cake 58–61
  frosted peanut butter cupcakes 122–125
  strawberry éclairs 74–77
  summer fruit tartlets 98–99
crème fraîche: caramel peach gateau 42–45
croissants 202–205
crown loaf 216–219
crusty white bread 172–175
cupcakes
  chocolate butterfly cupcakes 126–129
  double ginger cupcakes 132–135
  fairy cupcakes 130–131
  frosted peanut butter cupcakes 122–125

date, pistachio nut & honey slices 84–87
double chocolate mint sponge 36–37
double ginger cupcakes 132–135
dried fruit

cinnamon swirls 70–73
frosted carrot cake 58–61
mini florentines 164–167
spiced pear & sultana strudel 90–93

fairy cupcakes 130–131
fennel seeds: pumpkin & seed twist 192–195
feta & olive scones 200–201
filo pastry
  baklava 94–97
  chocolate filo parcels 78–79
  chocolate nut strudel 88–89
  spiced pear & sultana strudel 90–93
frosted carrot cake 58–61
frosted cherry rings 154–157

garlic: tomato tarte tatin 114–117
ginger
  crown loaf 216–219
  double ginger cupcakes 132–135
  mini florentines 164–167
golden syrup
  chocolate fudge cake 22–25
  chocolate nut strudel 88–89
  orange madeira ring 38–41

hazelnuts
  chocolate filo parcels 78–79
  chocolate hazelnut flapjack
    cookies 158–159
  crown loaf 216–219
honey
  baklava 94–97
  cherry & cinnamon tartlets 108–109
  honey & almond cake 46–47
  pumpkin & seed twist 192–195

irish soda bread 190–191

jam
  marzipan whirls 150–153
  victoria sponge cake 26–27

lemons
  apple danish 80–81
  apple streusel bars 56–57
  blueberry & passionfruit drizzle
    squares 52–55
  cherry & peel spirals 206–209
  chocolate butterfly cupcakes 126–129
  classic cherry cake 18–21

date, pistachio nut & honey slices 84–87
frosted cherry rings 154–157
honey & almond cake 46–47
lemon meringue pie 104–107
lemon poppy seed madeleines 140–141
polenta berry crunch buns 144–147
spiced pear & sultana strudel 90–93
low-fat blueberry muffins 136–139

macadamia nuts: apricot, macadamia &
  white chocolate chunk muffins 142–143
maple syrup
  caramel peach gâteau 42–45
  cinnamon swirls 70–73
marzipan whirls 150–153
mascarpone cheese: strawberry éclairs 74–77
mini florentines 164–167
mint
  chocolate filo parcels 78–79
  double chocolate mint sponge 36–37
mixed peel
  cherry & peel spirals 206–209
  crown loaf 216–219
mixed spice: baklava 94–97
muffins
  apricot, macadamia & white chocolate
    chunk muffins 142–143
  low-fat blueberry muffins 136–139

nutmeg: frosted carrot cake 58–61
nuts
  apple streusel bars 56–57
  apricot, macadamia & white chocolate
    chunk muffins 142–143
  baklava 94–97
  chocolate chip brownies 62–65
  chocolate filo parcels 78–79
  chocolate fudge cake 22–25
  chocolate hazelnut flapjack
    cookies 158–159
  chocolate nut strudel 88–89
  classic cherry cake 18–21
  coffee & walnut roulade 48–51
  crown loaf 216–219
  date, pistachio nut & honey slices 84–87
  frosted carrot cake 58–61
  frosted peanut butter cupcakes 122–125
  honey & almond cake 46–47
  marzipan whirls 150–153
  mini florentines 164–167
  rich almond cake 32–35

spiced pear & sultana strudel 90–93
summer fruit tartlets 98–99

oats
  chocolate hazelnut flapjack
    cookies 158–159
  classic oatmeal biscuits 148–149
olives
  feta & olive scones 200–201
  pesto & olive soda bread 180–181
onions
  broccoli, pancetta & blue cheese
    galette 110–113
  spring onion & parmesan
    cornbread 182–185
oranges
  baklava 94–97
  cinnamon spiced orange
    beignets 210–211
  frosted carrot cake 58–61
  orange madeira ring 38–41
oregano: tomato tarte tatin 114–117

pancetta: broccoli, pancetta & blue cheese
  galette 110–113
passionfruit: blueberry & passionfruit drizzle
  squares 52–55
pastries, savoury
  asparagus prosciutto wraps 118–119
  broccoli, pancetta & blue cheese
    galette 110–113
  tomato tarte tatin 114–117
pastries, sweet
  apple danish 80–81
  baklava 94–97
  chocolate filo parcels 78–79
  chocolate nut strudel 88–89
  cinnamon swirls 70–73
  date, pistachio nut & honey slices 84–87
  spiced pear & sultana strudel 90–93
  strawberry éclairs 74–77
  *see also* pies & tarts
peaches: caramel peach gateau 42–45
peanut butter: frosted peanut butter
  cupcakes 122–125
pears: spiced pear & sultana strudel 90–93
peppers: stromboli with salami, roasted
  peppers & cheese 196–199
pesto
  asparagus prosciutto wraps 118–119
  pesto & olive soda bread 180–181

pies & tarts
  apple pie 100–103
  cherry & cinnamon tartlets 108–109
  lemon meringue pie 104–107
  summer fruit tartlets 98–99
pine nuts
  baklava 94–97
  broccoli, pancetta & blue cheese
    galette 110–113
  cranberry & pine nut biscotti 160–163
pistachio nuts
  baklava 94–97
  chocolate chip brownies 62–65
  date, pistachio nut & honey slices 84–87
plaited poppy seed bread 176–179
polenta berry crunch buns 144–147
poppy seeds
  lemon poppy seed madeleines 140–141
  plaited poppy seed bread 176–179
prosciutto: asparagus prosciutto
    wraps 118–119
pumpkin & seed twist 192–195

rich almond cake 32–35
ricotta cheese
  double ginger cupcakes 132–135
  rich almond cake 32–35
rye bread 186–189

saffron: chocolate & saffron
    brioches 212–215
salami: stromboli with salami, roasted
    peppers & cheese 196–199
scones
  feta & olive scones 200–201
  plain scones 220–221
seeds, edible
  baklava 94–97
  broccoli, pancetta & blue cheese
    galette 110–113
  cinnamon squares 66–67
  cranberry & pine nut biscotti 160–163
  lemon poppy seed madeleines 140–141
  mini florentines 164–167
  plaited poppy seed bread 176–179
  pumpkin & seed twist 192–195
sesame seeds: baklava 94–97
small cakes and bars
  apple streusel bars 56–57
  apricot, macadamia & white chocolate
    chunk muffins 142–143

blueberry & passionfruit drizzle
    squares 52–55
chocolate butterfly cupcakes 126–129
chocolate chip brownies 62–65
double ginger cupcakes 132–135
fairy cupcakes 130–131
frosted peanut butter cupcakes 122–125
lemon poppy seed madeleines 140–141
low-fat blueberry muffins 136–139
marzipan whirls 150–153
polenta berry crunch buns 144–147
soured cream
  banana coconut loaf cake 28–31
  chocolate filo parcels 78–79
  cinnamon squares 66–67
spiced pear & sultana strudel 90–93
spring onion & Parmesan cornbread 182–185
strawberries
  strawberry éclairs 74–77
  victoria sponge cake 26–27
stromboli with salami, roasted peppers &
    cheese 196–199
summer fruit tartlets 98–99
sunflower seeds
  cinnamon squares 66–67
  mini florentines 164–167
  pumpkin & seed twist 192–195

tangerines: double ginger cupcakes 132–135
tomatoes
  feta & olive scones 200–201
  tomato tarte tatin 114–117

victoria sponge cake 26–27

walnuts
  baklava 94–97
  coffee & walnut roulade 48–51
  frosted carrot cake 58–61

yogurt
  cherry & cinnamon tartlets 108–109
  low-fat blueberry muffins 136–139

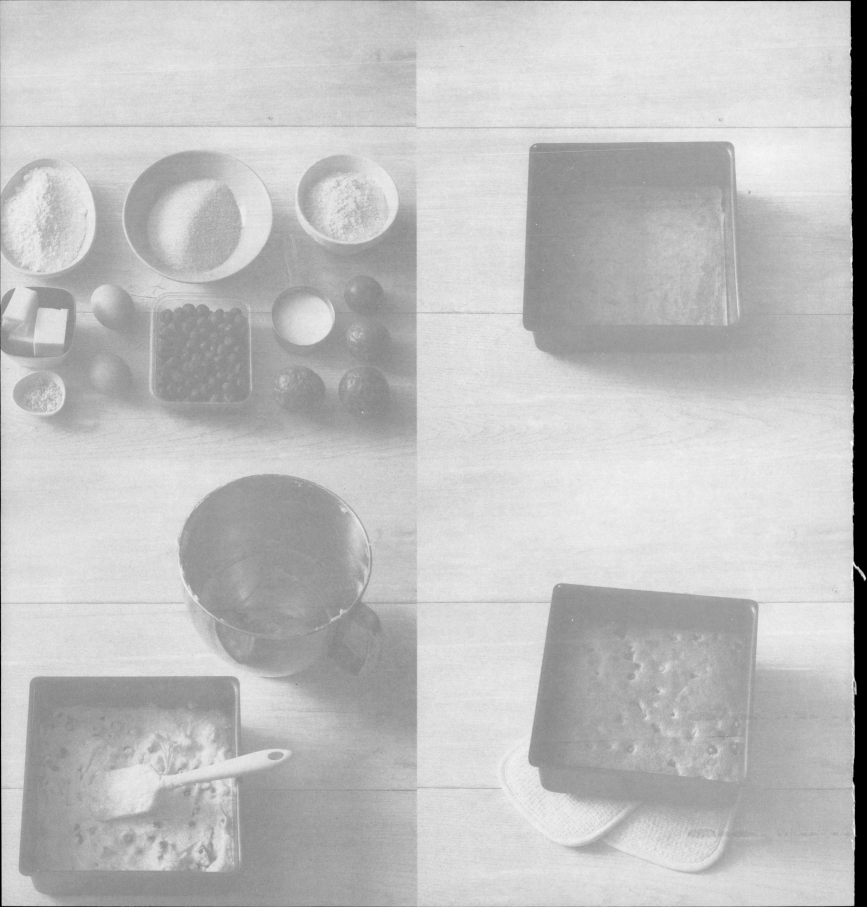